CHILDREN, DEATH & BEREAVEMENT

PAT WYNNEJONES

SCRIPTURE UNION
130 City Road, London EC1V 2NJ

© Pat Wynnejones 1985

First published 1985
Reprinted 1986

ISBN 0 86201 237 6

Printed and bound in Great Britain by
Ebenezer Baylis & Son Limited,
The Trinity Press, Worcester, and London.

Contents

Foreword

Childhood is the beginning of life, and, in the natural order of things, would seem to be as far removed from death as could be. Yet in fact there are many cases where the cradle and the grave are fearfully close. Some children do die, and some experience through death the loss of a mother, father, brother or sister, or other relative or friend.

Whatever neat theories we may hold about the best age at which to let the child become aware of death, whether through the teaching of the home or of the school, the stark realities make us realise that some children, and even very small children, find that death enters their experience. We may be those who have to help such children. What shall we do?

Many will feel deeply grateful to Pat Wynnejones for this book. Possibly there is nothing startlingly new in it. But that is one of its virtues. There is no attempt to produce bright new solutions to dark age-long problems. Much wisdom lies scattered about among many people, and here it is gathered together and made available to those who need it. The qualifications of the writer are her broad experience as mother, teacher, trainer of teachers and Christian, together with a careful and industrious investigation, not just into what has been previously written on the subject, but into actual human experiences. So the reader will feel constantly in touch with reality.

Many Christians have succumbed to Marxist ridicule of the Christian hope, and indeed certainty, about the world to come, and have therefore thought and spoken far too little about it. That is one reason why death is perhaps a bigger problem for Christians now than in the past: they have lost their truly Christian perspective. This book may help to restore that perspective. It does not attempt to give theological answers to all the profound questions – that would be beyond its scope – but it does breathe a deep faith and a proper humility before the mysteries which are hidden in the wisdom of God.

"Is my gloom, after all,
Shade of His hand, outstretched caressingly?"

That was the tentative realisation of Francis Thompson as he depicted in "The Hound of Heaven" the way God's love had been pursuing him. It was a mature faith which could see the deep sorrows and distresses of life not as the absence, but as the presence, of God.

Kenneth G. Howkins
Senior Lecturer in Religious Studies
Hertfordshire College of Higher Education

Preface

'Sorry I'm late, miss. My sister was electrocuted this morning!'

The classroom door had opened suddenly in the middle of a lesson being taken by one of my students on teaching practice. Later that day when she came for her tutorial she told me about the white-faced little boy's distress and about her own predicament. 'I didn't know what to do,' she complained, 'Well – what could I say?'

She felt that students' training should include some guidelines about how to deal with such a situation, or at least some idea of how children's understanding of death develops, and their possible reactions to it.

This made me think. It seemed to me that the student had a point. She started my interest in the subject, but it was not until several years later that I had the opportunity to pursue it as I wished; and to collect material from schools and institutions, and from many individuals who have been close to children who had suffered the loss of a parent. The purpose of the book is to share with any who have the interests of children at heart, the ideas and experiences of teachers, parents and children who have written or talked with me, or expressed their thoughts in drawing.

One correspondent wrote:

My father was killed at work by falling off a ladder when I was nearly seven years old. My parents were both committed Christians.

When my dad died, to me he had gone to be with Jesus – and that realisation made a big difference to me.

My mother encouraged us to continue to mention dad in our 'God bless . . .' prayers. This helped to reinforce the concept of dad not being dead but being alive with Jesus. As far as I can remember I dropped mentioning him when I realised he was OK with Jesus.

When my eldest brother's wife died of cancer two years ago, I wrote a story, 'The Journey', as I wanted to help his children (aged 13, 11, 10) to cope with the situation. The idea was partly geared to help the 11-year-old daughter as she was initially very upset about the thought of the body in the coffin. The story seemed to help them – and others who knew the family were also helped by it at the time. The concept is based on 2 Corinthians 5, verses 1–10.

The Journey

They had been travelling together for some time – a little group on a special journey. They each had a tent in which to live – and their tents were of different shapes and sizes – each having its own unique character and individual beauty. Each day the group pitched their tents a little nearer to their destination – a place they could not see – but which was going to hold for them more than all the experiences of the journey put together.

The group had begun with two people – or perhaps I should say three – since when they had lived on their own in the open countryside, the two, at different times, had met the Master of the Journey. He had pointed them in the direction of the destination, and from the day of this meeting he went with each of them on the journey. When on the way these two met each other, they decided to pitch their tents together. Three more soon joined their group and from then on their five tents were pitched side by side.

A time came when the tent of one of the first two began to be a problem for her and the journey became difficult. Some work was done to try to mend her tent but there was little improvement, and the fabric of her tent seemed to be wearing out. The others in the group talked to the Master of the Journey about the situation. They knew that he was able to restore worn out tents and that he loved them all very much. The Master knew that it was best for the group not to tell them all his plans at once, so they continued their journey with him, wondering what the future would hold. As time passed the failing tent became more and more difficult to live in, and the one who lived there needed a new living-place free from the suffering of the tent. It was not that she minded the journey – in fact she loved travelling with the rest of the group – but she knew that what awaited them at the end of the journey was something to look forward to very much.

One morning, something very special happened. The one

whose tent had now got to the point when it was becoming impossible to live in, looked out – and saw that instead of being on open ground (as her tent had been throughout the journey) it was inside a magnificent house. The room was set out in a way that perfectly suited her and she felt very much at home. From inside her tent she saw standing in the room her greatest friend – the Master of the Journey. She could now see him in a way she never had before. She realised that now inside the house she did not need the tent any longer. The Master of the Journey reached out his hand to her and she went quietly from the tent into her own room in the Master's home. What joy to be there with him!

The one whose tent had been pitched next to hers since they joined together did not see the room, or the house, or the Master. These are all invisible to those who are still on the journey. All that was there to be seen was that the tent was now empty and that the one whose tent it had been was no longer there. The group knew where she had gone – her journey was over – she had arrived at the Master's home. With her own special room there she had no more need of the tent.

It was difficult for the group to know how to think about the tent now. In one way it was very special as it had been the tent in which the one they loved had always lived. Yet the tent was not the person – and now that she was no longer visible to them, the tent was only worn out fabric which was no longer needed. The tent was carefully packed away; and the group along with many friends who were also heading for the same destination as they were, got together to say, 'Thank You' to the Master of the Journey for giving them such a lovely person and to rejoice together that the Master of the Journey loved them all so much and that he was guiding them all towards the enjoyment of his home.

The little group then continued their journey together. It was strange for them as they moved on with their tents no longer to have beside theirs the tent of the one who meant so much to them. But in some ways it was as if she was with them as she had always been, because there was much that was lovely in each of them, and in the life of their group, which came from the love she had given each of them and the special way she had cared for them all.   *Graeme C. Young*

Acknowledgements

My thanks are due to many who have been generous with their time, their advice and their experience.

I am particularly grateful to Kenneth Howkins Esq., MA, BD, Senior Lecturer in Religious Studies at Hertfordshire College of Higher Education, who has given me encouragement, the benefit of his wisdom on a number of difficult issues and permission to quote from his work.

Dr Janet Goodall, Consultant Paediatrician at the City General Hospital, Stoke-on-Trent (North Staffordshire Health Authority), too, has read and commented very helpfully on the manuscript, and has allowed me to quote from her book, *Suffering in Childhood*.

Many others have helped me in their different ways, among whom I am indebted to: Miss Elisabeth Earnshaw-Smith, Principal Social Worker at St Christopher's Hospice; Mr Derek Nuttall, Director of CRUSE, for allowing me to make use of CRUSE literature; Miss Myra Chave-Jones, psychotherapist and former Director of Care and Counsel; Miss Hazel Turner, the Headmistress, and pupils of St Paul's C of E Nursery, Infant and Junior School, Mill Hill; Mr Unsworth, the Headmaster, and pupils of Frith Manor Primary School, Woodside Park, London.

I would like to thank Gollancz Publishers and Alfred A. Knopf Inc. for permission to quote from *How It Feels When a Parent Dies*, by Jill Krementz and Mr Graeme C. Young for permission to use his story, 'The Journey'.

I have had many moving letters from bereaved parents. They wrote out of their pain, and I thank them because the book is richer for their contribution. 'I feel it is God's will that we should share our experiences', wrote one of them in the hope that their experience of sorrow might be a help to others and their children in similar distress. That is my hope too.

All the illustrative material in the book has been quoted verbatim from real life but the names have been altered.

1

The discovery of death

Children come across death naturally in a variety of ways. It is good to be open and honest with children in such experiences, and to help them to see a wholesome picture of death as a part of life.

As members of a sinful race all men die. (1 Corinthians 15: 22 Phillips)

'Men fear death as children fear to go in the dark' wrote Bacon, and for men and for children the basic causes of that fear are still the same. Both death and darkness present a mystery. What do they hold? What does the darkness hide? What awaits us in death? We cannot see the familiar scenes and well-loved faces to comfort and reassure us. The old Morality play, *Everyman*, tells our story. When we reach the end of life we have to leave behind everything that made it precious, home and family, friends and pleasures, and even good deeds.

Christians share some of that perplexity in facing the unknown, but they do have the comfort of knowing that they are not alone. 'Even when walking through the dark valley of death I will not be afraid, for you are close beside me, guarding, guiding all the way.' (Psalm 23:4, *The Living Bible*) It is knowing that we have a companion who has trod the way before us and will meet us at its end that takes away the sting. An old lady who had been lying unconscious for many hours suddenly opened her eyes with an expression of great joy and held out her arms. 'My Lord!' she cried, and fell back dead. In her helpful book *On Death and Dying*,[1] Dr Kuhbler-Ross tells of a terminally ill patient who did not share the universal fear of death. He knew, he said, that he was going to meet his Lord.

There is nothing very mysterious about death in a biological sense. We go back to dust. But nearly all peoples and all religions have believed that we are more than our chemical components. In the Aeneid Virgil gives a dismal picture of the departed spirits gathered on the banks of the River Styx, waiting to be ferried over to the kingdom of the dead. The Egyptians slaughtered the horses and slaves of dead Pharaohs, in case they should be needed in another life, and for the same reason the Viking chieftains had their treasures and their weapons buried with them. According to some beliefs we return from death in a different form, human or animal, according to how we have lived on earth. These are all essentially materialistic ideas. But the Bible teaches that we have only the one life on earth, and that what follows is in another dimension.

The Christian belief is that the evidence of our senses cannot tell us all that there is to know either about life or about death, for the spiritual dimension which is beyond our perceptions is none the less as real as this one. In one sense death has no meaning for those who have placed their trust in Jesus Christ, for they are in everlasting fellowship with God – a fellowship which is eternal, continuing throughout this life, through death and throughout life after death. At death we leave behind our physical being, together with our human concepts of space and time. We are more than limbs that fail and arteries that clog up: we are spiritual beings, body and spirit making up the total unique personality.

The separation of body and spirit that we call death was never part of God's original intention. It has come about as a result of mankind's rebellion. But God's love still reaches out to his alienated creation, offering restoration. It was for this that Jesus Christ died on a cross and rose as victor over death. Through faith in him we may be united with him in this life, and after death we may become like him and able to recognise one another in our resurrected and transfigured bodies.

This good news is the only answer to the separation of death, for we love people's bodies, with all their imperfections. They are the expression of their personality.

Although death is a natural part of life, we should not trivialise it when talking to children. It is not prosaic. It is not in the same order as shopping in the supermarket. To cheapen its solemnity is to give children a lie. Even at a young age children associate death with sadness. A six-year-old was looking at a dead tadpole in a classroom tank. 'How sad,' she said, 'it can't be with its friends any more.' She had expressed a basic truth. For it is the separation that makes death so fearful, and it is only the hope of reunion which can counter this fear.

For children the idea of reunion with their parents can be a real source of comfort in bereavement. The true hope, however, is not only that we shall be reunited with friends and relatives, but that we shall see Christ. A four-year-old who has been brought up to trust in Jesus can understand this. David, aged four, said, 'If you die you can go to Jesus.'

Separation

We are born into the world with an instinct to survive, to stay alive, to struggle against this enemy, death. Even a tiny baby will strive to float and not to drown. We are born with the instinct to survive – but the fear which accompanies this instinct is the fear of loss, the fear of separation from the mother. The way in which mother and father respond to baby's early needs – with speed and warmth and sensitivity – will influence the growing child's attitudes throughout life. A great deal of cuddling, rocking and contact comfort will help to combat those fears of loss and separation which are so dominant during the early months of life. A mother soon learns to distinguish between an angry cry, a hungry cry and a cry that simply asks for company. But the attention-seeking cry should never be allowed to become a cry of fear and panic. For the sense of trust that is nurtured when an infant is sure that someone who cares is near at hand is a first basic step in equipping that infant to cope with separation and bereavement whether these occur in childhood or in adult life.

Feelings of trust (or on the other hand of insecurity in a neglected child) are a significant element in the development of personality. These early experiences of being valued, or on the other hand of being rejected, make a great difference to the way in which a child learns to regard death, and to how he reacts to separation.

In a novel unfinished at the time of his death, Aldous Huxley has described an experience which is typical of the way in which a boy may become aware of himself as a living person who will one day inevitably have to die. He has been given a new airgun for his birthday and is out in the garden 'in a world of fantasy where I was stalking tigers, Boers, rhinoceroses, Redskins. Bang! Bang! Bang!' He takes potshots at various objects including sparrows, which fly away unharmed. Then he spots a chaffinch, which he means to scare away, but not to kill. Aiming vaguely in its direction, he lets fly and the bird falls to the ground like a stone. One moment it had been alive – the next it was dead.

> The chaffinch was lying there on the bare ground . . . Those tiny claws reaching reaching up toward the sky . . . I raised my hand and looked at it because it belonged to a living creature. But one day that creature would die. This moving, feeling hand would be no more than an appendage to a corpse. What was I? I was someone who was going to die.

He has made the connection between the universal fact of death and his own unique mortality.

Long before that momentous discovery, a child would have come upon death in many and various forms. It is natural to be curious about the little fledgling in the playground, fallen from the nest in spring. Why is it lying still, when other birds are hopping or flying? The toddler who treads on an ant or a worm is not displaying some sadistic tendency: she is making a discovery. Children will be concerned and earnest in their funeral arrangements for any dead creatures that they light upon – hedgehogs and sparrows, goldfish and mice. The burial fulfils a primitive need for ritual. Care will be taken in the selection of the shoebox or the chocolate box, the wrapping of the tiny form in leaves or cotton wool, maybe the binding of sticks to make a little cross, perhaps a prayer. Something is felt to be necessary and fitting. An event of significance has occurred and the demise of this furry or feathered creature must not pass without decent notice, especially of course if it is a beloved pet. Through such experiences children learn that death happens to every living creature and that suffering comes into every life.

Cycle of life

Children's awareness of death as a biological fact, as well as their opinions about life and death and what may or may not follow after, will vary according not only to age and intellectual development but also in respect of family background and belief. They form their attitudes and opinions from what they observe as well as what they are taught, and children from different backgrounds will have different ideas as to what is involved in saying that a person is dead.

For a child living in the country death may be a more familiar, less remote affair than it may be for the town child. It is part of the order of things. The constant process of renewal, the fact that while each winter blots out the living world in white, each summer brings new growth, must make a deep though maybe not conscious impression. Death is no stranger on the farm.

The seasons do not fail, the seed is sown, the harvests gathered. God can be trusted. He has ordered things well, and death comes into the plan. Behavioural problems seem to be less in rural districts. Security may play an important role in this; and it can also affect attitudes towards death and bereavement. The country life is not only seen, it is experienced; the child's perceptions of the rhythms of existence are attuned to the life cycles of animals and insects, plants and birds.

Framework for living

Children who grow up within the Church family enjoy a similar advantage of living within a framework which imparts security, a child's basic need in loss or separation. Picture to yourself a church with its ancient pews where generation after generation has sat: the whispering children have become attentive parents, then nodding grandparents, making way at last for the next generation of children. They in their turn watch the swallow flit past the stained glass window, wonder at the stone knight asleep on his stone tomb and read the brasses recalling dead loved ones. We live; we die; others follow on. It's natural. It's right.

In town or country children who grow up in the Christian

framework become attuned to the pattern of baptism or dedication, wedding, funeral and all that they can mean. They participate in the festivals; they love to gather round the Christmas crib and share the joy of the Baby's birth; they join in wondering sorrow to learn that 'Jesus died for all the children': they rejoice that he came to life and is still alive; they delight in the Easter garden and its gold and purple crocuses: they hear that there is life everlasting and Heaven is their home.

It is surprising that the inestimable benefits of the Church year as a national institution have hardly been recognised even by those with the interests of growing children at heart. There has been little protest as we become increasingly secular, watching our heritage eroded by the pressures of expediency and humanist or political interest. Isolated and meaningless Bank Holidays do not help children to perceive a pattern in life, in the way that religious festivals do.

Taboo

It has been remarked, ironically, that sex, which was taboo to the Victorians, has become our preoccupation, while death, which they regarded with equanimity, has until recently been the taboo of the twentieth century. Would 'death education' be as effective as sex education has proved? For we have been made aware that psychiatric problems can be caused by our reticence. The comparison is unrealistic: after all, this is not something that children can grow up looking forward to! No, by its nature it is something we shun and find hard to talk about. This may be partly due to the fact that death so rarely occurs in the home nowadays. One result of medical advance and the welfare state is that death has been distanced from our thinking, and its remoteness has added to its terror.

Close and real

In past generations there were few families who did not lose a member at an early age through hard childbirth, infant complaints and epidemics. The literature of the time, which is so full of deathbed scenes, simply records the way life was. In particular the children of the industrial city were victims of neglect, illness, semi-starvation, poor sanitation. Many of them died in infancy, and the desperate plight of slum families is depicted by writers such as Mrs. Gaskell, Charles Dickens and Silas Hocking.

In *Little Meg's Children* by Hesba Stretton, a common practice of the time is brought before our eyes. When the mother dies, the children spend a day and night with her body. Such delayed funerals were not only customary, they were proper, rather than to hurry the deceased into the grave.

One writer of the period tells how her mother took her to see a neighbour who had given birth to a stillborn child. The visit, even for a little girl, was socially correct, showing a proper concern. The dead baby was in an ordinary cardboard box on a washstand in the bedroom. She went over and peeped at the tiny form and touched the little waxlike cheek and fingers. She did not feel revulsion, anxiety or fear, but only wonder.

Invalids then were nursed with or without success at home, whereas now hospitalisation is the usual practice; and old people came to the end of their days by their own fireside instead of being hustled into institutions or lonely lodgings like so many of today's senior citizens. For today's children this is unfortunate: not only does it deprive them of the extended family framework, the security and patience of the older generation, but it denies them a natural introduction to the way we all have to leave this world for eternity.

Their way may have been harsh, but it was realistic.

Remote and plastic

Probably most of today's children have their ideas about death shaped by the unreal and hardening world of television violence.

It would be quite possible for them to see several killings during the course of one night's viewing if a parent is not exercising control over the knobs. So much violent death must encourage a false view of life. It is highly probable that the killings may be carried out with a degree of sadism that could make a damaging imprint on the mind of the viewer, especially during the impressionable years of childhood. It is the manner of presentation that matters.

For instance, Robin Hood died nobly at the end of the last series I saw. It was well handled for children, suggesting in the flight of the outlaw's last arrow that a courageous soul had finally sped on its way. There is a great difference between charging armies seen at a distance and a close-up of a knife being slowly drawn across a throat. Lots of courage and little blood should be the keynote. The sight of cowboys rolling off a roof in a gunfight is less harmful than a single concentrated scene of deliberate cruelty.

There is even a sense in which it can be helpful to portray certain deaths – these are the deaths of the villains in films such as 'Dr. Who' and 'Star Wars' or of the baddies in the old-style Westerns where the victory of the hero leaves a sense of justice and moral satisfaction. The characters in such films have a symbolic function representing goodness and evil, like the witches and dragons and knights of fairy-tale. Like them they make a useful contribution to a child's understanding when trying to define and clarify ideas about justice and morality.

And what about Tom and Jerry? How confusing are these cartoons for someone with only a few years' experience of the world? Do they believe that a creature who has been flattened by a steamroller may spring up again to throw a smart custard pie at his opponent?

I was pleasantly reassured by the following conversation with a small group of little children in the local primary school:

Q:	What happens to people when they die?
Alison (6):	They go up to heaven.
Q:	Do you know Tom and Jerry?
Peter (5):	No.
Andrew (5):	Yes. They're a cartoon. And sometimes they're sort of pretending to be dead.
Q:	They pop up again?
Andrew (5):	They're really just pretending that they're dead.
Alison (6):	Sometimes in films people die because there's a sword stuck in them, but they're not really dead. They're probably plastic toys.
Andrew (5):	They're sort of acting, but really somebody makes the film, so nobody's really dead.

There doesn't seem to be much confusion in the minds of these children. They are clear about the differences between the plastic world and the real one. This is all the more impressive considering that they are still in some doubt about the difference between animate and inanimate objects, as we shall see later.

It is encouraging to see that the BBC takes very seriously criticism of their children's programmes. The producer of one children's series defended the showing of an episode in which a pupil was drowned during a school swimming session. He made it clear that much thought had gone into the decision to show the incident as to how it should be presented. It was to be a warning against fooling around while swimming, an opportunity to view death objectively and to see its effect on others.

Horror

Unfortunately the Reports of the Parliamentary Group Video Enquiry revealed that a surprisingly high proportion of children from the age of seven watch video nasties and are therefore likely to have their idea of death coloured by these gruesome pictures. Their discovery of death will be associated with horror, sadism and fear. Or sitting up late to watch TV, they may witness someone being lynched, or a close-up of the victim being strangled, knifed or kicked to death.

Death may be forever tinged with evil and the occult for those children who have watched the late night horror film with its ghosts, skeletons, werewolves, corpses arising from the graves and churchyard Black Magic practices. At a vulnerable age children may have images of death imprinted on the mind as indescribably terrifying. An eight-year-old could not sleep without nightmares for many nights after seeing such a video at a friend's house.

The problem is not one of confusion between the real world and the plastic one, but of the way in which the representations of the screen may affect the child's feelings about the real fact and experience.

Beauty

We live in a society which makes status symbols of youth and beauty, and undervalues the qualities which may enhance old age. The focus of our concern is the beginning of life, not its ending. I wonder how many films I have seen of the birth of a baby, shown rightly as something beautiful. But the TV news coverage shows constant repellent pictures of death as the result of famine, war and natural disaster. There are some few photographers and painters who have captured the beauty of old age (Whistler's portrait of his mother, for instance), and there are poets who have seen death, not as a 'grim reaper' but as a gentle sleep or as a friend. 'Life is perfected by death' wrote Elizabeth Barrett Browning.

I smiled to think God's greatness flowed around our
    incompleteness, –
Round our restlessness, His rest. (*Rime of the Duchess May*)

And this is how it should be, for the dead landscape of winter can be even more ethereally beautiful in its white purity than the lush splendour of summer green. Bare black branches make intricate splendid patterns in silhouette against the sky, and skeleton leaves display the perfection of their geometric design. Dead grasses and the translucent 'pennies' of honesty decorate our homes when there are no live flowers to be found.

Death need not be ugly. Beauty is in the eye of the beholder. Those who came to see my mother after she had died saw peace and beauty, dignity, sweetness and calm. In *The Hiding Place*, Corrie Ten Boom tells how she peeped into the sick bay at Ravensbruck and saw Betsy's body lying there. The ravages of ill-treatment and deprivation had been wiped out by death and her natural loveliness restored.

Although many people nowadays prefer to request that money should be sent to missions and charities in remembrance of the one they loved, yet there is a place, too, for making funerals as beautiful with flowers as Christians like to make them joyful with music and hymns. In spite of the prevailing humanist ethos in which we live and the gloom with which death is regarded, a Christian death is always an occasion for hope, for the re-affirmation of faith and for joy in the presence of the Lord. It can even be so for the death of a child. Timothy died of leukaemia when he was ten. His parents chose to sing

> Praise Him, Praise Him,
> Praise Him in the morning,
> Praise Him when the sun goes down.
>
> Trust Him, trust Him,
> Trust Him in the morning,
> Trust Him when the sun goes down.

2
The Understanding of Death

As children grow they develop physically and mentally. As they pass through different stages of development they will grow in their discovery and understanding of death among other things. It is helpful to be aware of these stages and to respond appropriately; above all to provide an environment of love and security.

It's like this: when I was a child I spoke and thought and reasoned as a child does. 1 Corinthians 13:11 (The Living Bible)

Children are used to asking questions and getting satisfactory answers. They do it all the time. But the questions they may ask when they lose someone to whom they have been deeply attached are different. They are different, in the first place, because we do not have the answers. We do not know why death should sometimes strike suddenly at the young and strong, nor what precisely happens at death and after. They are also different because the answers needed are less to satisfy the mind than to afford some kind of comfort to the heart.

Such answers as we can give may be some help, but the response of a child to the experience of bereavement will depend on many factors: whether the death was the result of a sudden accident or followed a long illness, whether he has been brought up within a framework of Christian belief and what is

21

his understanding of the meaning of death. This understanding may include both the biological and the spiritual aspects: that is, both acceptance that death is final as far as the body is concerned, and realisation that there is more in the make-up of the human being than the body; and this cannot dawn until the child has reached some concept of himself as a person separate from those around.

Peep-Bo

To accept the personal implication, as, for instance, in Aldous Huxley's boyhood realisation that he 'was a creature who was going to die', must first require knowledge of oneself as an individual. A little baby has no such understanding. In the first weeks of life mother and baby comprise a unit. They are inseparable. Gradually the baby begins to gain a sense of selfhood, to smile in the expectation of eliciting a response, to turn the head towards a parent's voice. From three months old babies enjoy and learn from the game of Peep-bo. As mummy or daddy appears smiling over the cot, disappears, then re-appears again, the baby confirms his sense of individuality and is acquainted with the idea of being and non-being.

When he sits up in his high chair the child finds other ways of experimenting with being and non-being. He throws his spoon on the floor, and when you pick it up he throws it down again . . . and again . . . and again! It has gone. It comes back. Then he puts his spoon under the plate. 'All gone,' he says. He eats his dinner. 'All gone!' He waves goodbye to Daddy. 'All gone, Daddy,' he says – but Daddy will come back again. People go as well as things, but usually both things and people do return. The learning process involves various means of experimentation, and often we have to fish many of those 'all gone' things out of the loo!

As he becomes more conscious of his own identity, from about a year old, the child becomes more anxious about being separated from his mother, and, especially the two-year-old, will become very distressed if mother goes out of sight. He may not like being held by other people, and a loud howl will accompany Mummy's departure from the room. This is a particularly unfortunate age for a child to lose mother, the first person with whom the powerful process of bonding has been formed, for although not aware of death, the child is very

22

aware of separation. This separation anxiety is indeed the primary characteristic of the age.

Becoming myself

In becoming conscious of being his own self, the two-year-old has also discovered a powerful force in his will, and that he can impose it on his parents by certain ploys. He will spend all the air in his lungs in 'trying it on', and quickly learns that meals and potty training times can be used to manipulate Mummy; that the threat of a screaming fit in a public place will soon bring Daddy to heel. Temper tantrums, characteristic of the 'Terrible Twos' are a good way of finding out just how far he can go, how far he can control his world.

Although these discoveries may not appear to have any bearing on the understanding of death, they are part and parcel of the process by which a child builds a sense of trust and learns that his world is reliable. It is important that there should be discipline in the home, not rigid, but firm and consistent – no great swings from anger to indulgence and back. Security is built on finding that actions have predictable results, and a sense of security will help to equip the child for bereavement whether it should occur in childhood or in adult life.

The first years of life are full of curiosity about the world, which the toddler sees as revolving around himself. He looks to see what it contains, to find the names of things, to try their taste, to feel what they feel like. He also wants to know about the people in his life, and how he fits into the family framework.

Peter, at the age of two years four months, sorts out the family by sex: 'Daddy – boy, Mummy – girl,' he says. Then 'Jonathan – boy, Peter – boy.' Each child seeks to model himself or herself on the parent of the same sex. Emily (2) chooses the same occupations as her mother. She sees her hoovering and follows round with her sweeper. She baths and feeds her doll, changes her nappy and gives her pram rides. Peter chooses cars and trains and things with wheels. For Peter and Emily, typical of their age, are making themselves a picture of the person each hopes to be. This is so obviously a need in the lives of toddlers that their loss is great if either parent dies. A parent left alone needs help to find an appropriate father-figure or mother-figure from among relatives or close friends to fulfil the role of 'model' for them.

23

Dead or alive?

As the child becomes conscious of individuality and views the world from an objective standpoint, movement or lack of it will be among the most obvious things he will observe. This will become his criterion in assessing life or death. Death is what has happened to the canary on the floor of the cage. But he does not yet understand that it is permanent. In her book *On Death and Dying*, Dr Kuhbler-Ross mentions a small boy who said, 'I will bury my doggy now, and next spring when the flowers come up he will get up.'

We warn the children that if they play in the road they may be run over and killed, but small children understand this only hazily, perhaps as something resembling sleep, from which you will wake again. This may be illustrated from the play fantasies of children in the nursery school. They put their Lego men under cars, run over them and then bring them back to life. Similarly, in their games of cops and robbers, a few minutes of 'death' on the ground will do before they jump up and off again.

Children in the infant school gather conkers, leaves, shells and feathers, and grow seedlings on the nature table. They keep hamsters which may or may not survive. A good teacher will encourage talk as an aid to observation and reasoning about all this classroom provision. They listen to stories, some of which may contain incidental deaths, and to fairy tales such as Snow White, Beauty and the Beast and The Happy Prince, which allow the child to explore ideas about being and non-being, sleep and death. Through these experiences they acquire an impressive command of language, which gives them freedom and clarity in their thinking, and enables them to abstract the concept of death from the wide range of ideas and images.

> (Robin (4) and Adam (5) are looking at two twigs, one with dead leaves and one with new growth.)
>
> Adam: These leaves have died. These have not died and those are dead. Alive is when they stay a long time. Dead is when they don't stay.
>
> Q: What can you see in the room that is alive?
>
> Adam: Books, because we use them. Topsy and Tim (looking at book) are not really alive because they are not talking. They're just laughing and splashing about.

24

Q: What is the difference between Topsy and Tim
        and you and Robin?

Adam: We can walk and they can't.
        My little brother is alive but he's only a baby.
        (Presumably Adam is pointing out that although
        his brother cannot walk, it is because he is only a
        baby and not because he is a picture!)

Robin: Books are alive because people turn them.

Q: Are books alive? Is a car alive?

Robin and Adam: Yes. Because people drive it.

Adam: (Looking at picture) That's an old man and he's
        going to get dead.

Q: Do people die for other reasons than getting old?

Robin: Yes. Someone shot them.

Q: Are the sun and the moon alive?

Robin: Yes.

Q: Is that pen alive?

Robin: Yes. People write with it.

Q: Is my watch alive?

Robin: Yes, because it ticks.

Q: But if it stopped?

Robin: That means it's dead.

Asked if they could find anything dead in the room, Adam
trotted off and came back with two books in which there were
pictures of an actress lying on the stage and a very old man in a
Roman bath house.

A problem arises when talking with children of this age
about pictures. It is difficult to know whether by 'dead' they
mean that the characters in the book are only pictures (i.e. not
real people) or whether they mean that they are dead in the
story. We looked at a book in which there was a dead bird and
at one in which someone was acting dead.

Adam: She's going to be dead because the arrow is in her.

Robin: She's bleeding. It's sad to be dead, isn't it?

Adam: The bird is asleep.

Robin: That's dead, isn't it? (Robin was right. The bird in
        the picture was dead.)

Q: What is the difference between being asleep and
        being dead?

Adam: Because one's asleep and the others don't know

25

they're dead (i.e. people who are asleep know that they are.)

Robin: (pointing to picture of actress acting dead) She's dead.

Q: Will she ever get up again?

Robin: No, because she's dead.

Q: Can't you ever get up when you're dead?

Robin: (laughing at what he obviously considered a silly question) No!

Robin's reaction shows that it is possible for a four-year-old to grasp the finality of death as an objective fact, but that does not mean either that all four-year-olds would have done so, or that it would be accepted as a reality in any experience where he was emotionally involved.

Q: Why are we sad when people die?

Robin: Because someone shot them.

Q: But if they die when they're old?

Robin: (defensively) I don't know. My parents have not yet told me.

Even at a very young age many children seem to associate sadness with death (illustrated also by their pictures) or seem reluctant to think about it. Robin's picture clearly shows that he sees the difference between life and death as involving happiness as a characteristic of life and sadness of death. Ben refused to draw a picture of death 'because it was too sad'.

On the other hand, it is a subject of absorbing interest to others. Understanding of the biological aspects of death is likely to advance in line with other conceptual thinking. Older infants had no problem in identifying dead leaves, living plants, dried grasses and in explaining their criteria, e.g. 'these leaves are crumpled up,' 'these are straight'. Their observations will have helped them to realise that although some things are plainly dead there are also things that never have been alive. Five and six-year-olds can reason perceptively about whether a desk is alive or dead:

Q: Is this desk alive or dead?

Andrew (5):
Peter (5): } Dead
Alison (6):

William, 4 yrs 2 mths

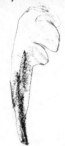 

a live tree

a dead tree
William is aware of seasonal
changes in regard to life and
death

Robin, 4 yrs 3 mths

*Daddy buried a dead squirrel in
a hole. It couldn't get out.*
Robin associates death with
absence of movement

a live squirrel can climb a tree

Ben, 4 yrs 4 mths

a dead hedgehog
Ben wouldn't draw a dead one
because it was not happy

a live hedgehog

Adam, 4 yrs 8 mths

dead   *alive*
                          happier to be alive

Simeon, 4 yrs 11 mths

dead   *alive*
he only wanted to draw the
alive one because it's nicer to
be alive

Alison 5 yrs 1 mth

a flower   *a dead flower*
I like live flowers   Alison does not like dead ones

28

Andrew (5):	Because it's made of wood
Q:	Where did the wood come from?
Alison (6):	Trees

Andrew (5):   It could have come from the bark of a tree, but they probably scraped the bark off first. Other things come from trees – benches that you sit on.

Children's ideas do not advance in an orderly, measurable progression. Their thinking ranges to and fro over various possibilities and they spark off thoughts as they talk in a small group, inspiring each other to consider all aspects of the subject. According to these children you would know whether or not a shellfish or a snail were alive because the shell would be empty if the occupant were dead, and a sea shell would change colour. Sunshine is alive because it is very hot and glasses are alive if they are helping someone to see, but shoes are dead because they only move if someone is wearing them. As you see, although these children exhibited considerable reasoning faculties, their argument carried some interesting illogicalities.

Kenneth Howkins has pointed out in conversation that at this age children recognise some characteristics of life and death, but cannot distinguish them precisely, and so may misapply them. Thus the simple logic may be that dead is still, and living is moving – so what moves is alive. Adults also can say that the engine of their car is 'dead', and there is no sign of life in it. Children do not always distinguish between the literal and metaphorical use of words. They may see separate characteristics of life, but not be able to group them together adequately.

Punishment or Kindness?

Children earnestly look for guidelines to help them sort out their ideas on the perplexing question of morality. Matters concerning classroom and playground justice, and whether decisions are 'fair' are of immense importance; and they look to stories where villains and heroes are clearly drawn to help them. This is not the age for subtleties of character. Heroes must truly embody their ideals; villains must merit their punishment. Later will come the time for true-to-life characterisation but at this stage it is more helpful to see films and read books in which the baddies get their deserts – maybe they are killed off. Here death is seen as punishment, the just reward for evil deeds:

Q:	Do you think it's always sad when people die?
Andrew (5):	Well, if they were baddies it wouldn't be sad, but if they were goodies it would be quite sad for people.
Alison (6):	If it was your family you would be sad, wouldn't you? Really really sad. If it was your mummy or daddy it would be so sad because if you were only five years and your mummy was old and she died . . .
Alison (6):	Some people die because they just have to. God wants them to die.
Andrew (5):	I think some people die because they may be bad people.
Q:	Do good people die, too?
Peter (5): Andrew (5): Alison (6):	} Yes.
Alison (6):	Sometimes he wants people to die because they might get ill soon.
Andrew (5):	Yes.
Alison (6):	If God makes you die before you're going to get ill it would be quite nice.

Sad or glad?

Primary age children readily identify with the sorrowful and the brave. They are looking for characters who portray human nature at its idealistic best on whom to model their own self-image, and they are ready for stories about courage and self-sacrifice. Here are the same young children exploring further the idea that death may not always be sad. Notice that with all the hesitation and imperfect expression, as well as the mistake about the manner of Christ's death, Calvary is linked in their minds with the heroism of the soldier who volunteered for death to save his comrades by 'admitting' to hiding a spade during the building of the bridge over the River Kwai:

Q: Do you think it's nice in heaven?

Andrew (5):   Well, yes, in a way it is because . . . because each Easter when he died a very long time ago . . . people shot him and then he was taken up to heaven. But he always is alive again because he's the King that lasts for ever.

Alison (6):   Mummy told me that God is everywhere.

Andrew (5):   Well, yes, he is really because he can be beside anybody at any time really.

Peter (6):   In a play at this school once there were some guards at a prison. They were very bad. And there were some people who had to be on the bridge and he said that there wasn't enough spades. There was. And he asked all the paraders, who had seen the spade and they all said 'all of them are there'. And one said 'It was I, sir,' but he just did that because he hadn't done it and he just really had taken his life . . .

Andrew (5):   He didn't really want his friends to die, so he really just made himself die . . .

Alison (6):   I think it is sad.

Peter (5):   So do I.

Andrew (5):   But he really gave up his life because no one had really taken the shovel. The guards had just counted the shovels wrongly . . . I think the man was a bit sad and a bit glad. Glad to have helped his friends and sad for himself to die.

Alison (6):   I think he was very brave. Anyway God would be kind to him if he went up there to heaven.

It is clearly a mature approach that can juxtapose the ideas of glad and sad as Andrew does, while Alison expresses a confident attitude, perhaps acquired from home or church.

Ideas from far and wide

In the Junior School, children's ideas will be influenced by the cultural mix in the area, as well as by their reading and television viewing. A television Middle English programme, 'Game of Soldiers' was followed by a discussion with 10–11 year olds, which produced the following thoughts: that it was better to die than to be dishonoured, and that death holds an escape route out of this world; and then followed very vague ideas of heaven or hell – or nothing. Oral discussion will spark off ideas, but thoughts are to a certain extent directed by the flow of conversation. Personal writing gives children more time to draw on their own resources. These pieces reveal that by this age children have given a surprising amount of thought to the subject.

> To think of its happening to me always mystifies me in many ways that I can't explain. It scares me when I am alone. To think of a life finishing as quick as a flash makes me wonder what will happen next. Will I have a new life as an animal or a life in a different dimension? Well, these are the questions I ask myself when I think of death. Since death is . . . death? Who knows?

They had a clear idea of biological death:

> Death is when the body stops functioning. All the major cells stop so the body stops too.

Several children mentioned the fact that death must be 'accepted' (e.g. 'Everything dies'), though this was by no means easy. This child, for instance, shows an understanding that death is the inevitable end to life, which is probably what he means by the phrase 'accepting it', but he is not reconciled to it, since he says, 'mostly I cry':

> When death comes people should learn to accept it because it always comes sooner or later. Death is nothing really to be afraid of. My mother doesn't accept death. She cries. I just go out of the room and wait for her to stop. Sometimes I accept death but mostly I cry. My dad accepts death and sometimes he gets in a temper. For me it's hard to accept death. I wish everybody could.

We can see in these writings how hard it is for children who are reaching out towards some answer to the mystery of death that will both allay their anxiety and offer comfort when they lose someone they love. The writer of the next piece is able, not only to view life and death objectively, but also to review his experience, and even to preview it, in the sense that, regretting his past behaviour, he will be in a position to act differently in future:

> Death is very depressing when the person who has died meant so much to you. Even when that person was unkind to you, somewhere in your heart, deep down, there is some sadness. I always feel sad and I sometimes wish I had been nicer to the person who has died.

There were several children who found comfort in the thought that the dead person would be at peace, though without expressing any explicit Christian belief on which to base that hope:

> Death is when somebody is resting peacefully forever. I think people should not be afraid of death. It is something we have to live with. We should not be scared of it. Death is when someone dies and you think, 'Oh, I will never see them again', but I think they have gone to a good home where they can rest in peace with no one to bother them. My Nan has been dead now for two years. It was a shock at first but I thought to myself, 'She has gone to a good home where she can rest in peace and when I die I shall meet her.'

Children of this age are keenly interested in justice and like to see the baddies get their deserts. More significant, however, is this child's realisation that it is possible to express a wish for someone to die without really meaning it. Such an understanding would help to relieve him of guilty feelings in the event of his father or mother actually dying:

> Death is sometimes nice and sometimes horrible. It is sometimes nice, for instance on a television programme you wish that the bad man could be dead, and often when your mum or dad tell you off you say to your selfish thought, 'I wish they were dead', but the only difference with wishing your mum or dad were dead is that you don't really mean it.

Young as they are, these children are beginning to form opinions about issues of life and death such as euthanasia which they will have heard discussed on the media:

33

Death can also be for the best. I think if somebody is in a great deal of pain then they should be put to sleep. If I was in a great deal of pain and I couldn't be healed I think I would prefer to be put to sleep rather than suffer the pain.

It was obvious that among these children real Christian teaching was scarce, though there were plenty of ideas picked up from the current humanistic mix, and among them reincarnation was popular:

I think when you die you go somewhere else for about fourteen years then you come back to earth.

Death could be the flowers in winter and almost like reincarnation when they grow again in spring. When I die I would like to be reincarnated. I'd like to come back as a wild horse roaming over wide open spaces and galloping across the moors and mountains, eating the sweet juicy grass and heather, drinking the crisp cold water of streams running from the top of the mountains.

From among sixty pieces of writing only one child expressed a firm belief that death means extinction:

I am Jewish and we are taught that there is a third world . . . my real view is that there is no third world, you just stop short. With this view I am extremely afraid of death.

By one means or another the others expressed their belief that death is not the end:

Death is like living, but your soul lives and your body is dead.

If someone in your family dies it has an effect on you. Christians believe that when you die your soul is still here.

By 'still here' the writer probably means simply that the 'soul' has not been extinguished. Children are capable of greater complexity of thought than they can express in words, and the child is trying to say that the person still exists, though 'here' does not necessarily mean on earth. Many of the children saw that what a person does in life has some bearing on what happens after death, and connected the thought of heaven or hell with reward or punishment for deeds on earth:

THE UNDERSTANDING OF DEATH

Death is when someone isn't alive any more and when they go to heaven or hell.

When you are dead you are not really dead because your body is still in its grave but the rest of you, called the soul, goes to heaven or hell.

When someone dies I think if they have been good and kind they go up to heaven.

After death people go to God. Then God asks what bad things we've done and what good things we've done through our lives. Then if the good things are more than the bad things we go to heaven, and if the bad things are more we go to hell. On our arms are two angels. On our right arm is a good angel who writes down all the good things we did, and on our left arm the bad angel writes down the bad things we did.

When you die you don't just rot away, your soul goes to heaven or hell.

The next extract seems to reflect a confusion of thought, but it may well be another problem of verbalisation. 'In heaven' may mean 'in the next life', whatever it should be, and that God makes his displeasure known in that afterlife.

If you have done bad things in your life God doesn't look after you well while you are in heaven.

The next writer, however, does appear to be genuinely confused (probably influenced by today's woolly liberalism) and sees no need for repentance and forgiveness:

When you die I think every human goes to heaven because God loves us all. I think death is slow and painful, but if you have been naughty you still go to heaven.

One child associated belief in God with goodness as the way to heaven:

Your soul goes to heaven if you believe in God and are good and your soul goes to hell if you worship the devil and are bad.

The devil was not often referred to, but some children showed evidence of being influenced by the obsession with the occult which is prevalent:

> After death people come back as ghosts. I think I am haunted.

> My view on death is life after death: ghosts, spirits, heaven or hell. Heaven: angels, people with wings on their backs who serve God. Hell: victims of evil, murderers burning in hell fire. Then living again, reincarnation, perhaps a horse or a chimpanzee could become a man again, perhaps people go to hell – maybe it is the world full of evil. That's my view on death.

An interesting idea expressed was that a death in the family gave an opportunity to the bereaved to make a fresh start in life:

> If someone dies in your family, pray to God your Saviour, let him be in your spirit and your soul, give your life to God and start a new life.

There were some imaginative accounts of what heaven might be like:

> I tried to think what would happen when you die. I thought that you would stop working, die, and then you would be buried and then be taken by angels up to a place which was very beautiful and peaceful. All the time you would be watching what's happening on earth. In this world would be all dead things like animals and people.

(It is not clear what is meant by 'this world', but probably it means an afterlife for animals as well as people.)

> Death is the calling from heaven, unhappiness for us but happiness for them. When you're doing something and all of a sudden the world just goes black, like you were in a cupboard and the door shut. Then you find yourself in a dark tunnel, only your heart guides you through the right tunnel. If you're evil you will just keep wandering through the tunnels. If you're good you will see a light at the end of the tunnel. When you get to the end of the tunnel there is a garden full of roses and daisies and all the flowers you can think of. There are lots of people playing in this wonderful

garden and there is no evil anywhere. When you have been up there for a century then you start your life all over again down on earth as a baby, and have a new mother and father.

This last is a graphic description of what the boy sees in store for him:

Death is a sensation of good and bad. Life with God or death with the Devil. I found myself falling at a great pace down a tunnel. Then I stopped as if a person had stopped a great lift with a metal lever. I saw a face that looked like Jesus. He opened a great book and said, 'What is your name?' I replied, 'Roger Bennett'. Jesus said, 'Your record is good, follow me.' We went through endless corridors until we came to a door which said 'TEST'. I entered and inside I saw a picture of Mr. Hughes, my teacher from primary school. The next picture was of Halford's in Putney for some reason, and a picture of my friends, Ranjan and Saleem. Then I saw Jesus who said, 'Go into heaven through the everlasting gates and into eternal life.'

There were also some stoics:

I wish there were no such thing as death, but we just have to put up with it.

We all have to die some day. Death is something we have to live with.

Death is a pain in the neck, when you think of it.

There is a naivete and assurance about some of these opinions that may make us smile, but their very earnestness makes it impossible for us to dismiss them lightly. They demonstrate that from the time children are ready to leave the primary school their minds are open to all the aspects of death that the adult mind can contemplate. For them death will have become part of a philosophical framework, seen with their fully developed concepts of time and space and the laws of cause and effect, as one of the predictable principles that govern the universe.

'When I became a man . . .'

The adolescent is no longer a child, nor yet fully mature. The world is a different world from that of childhood and demands a new sort of understanding. It is a time of questioning all that has been taught by parents, school and church. Christian children may find it particularly traumatic. They may be challenged by teachers who pour scorn on their beliefs and many of their friends may also be sceptics. School leavers will have to re-examine the spiritual truths and moral guidelines of their faith in the light of the secular society into which they have emerged. They may question the authority of the Bible, seen against the superficial attractiveness of prevailing situation ethics, for they are under pressure to conform to the permissive standards of their peer group. They may wonder if what the Bible has to say about miracles and about death is true. They will be asking adult questions. Is there really such a place or state as heaven? And is it for everyone? The study of comparative religion at school may have blurred the words of the Sunday school lessons. Is the idea of hell simply a hangover from medieval times? They are rubbing shoulders with those of other faiths and their ideas about what happens after death. Reincarnation has been given a good airing on radio and television in recent years. What about yoga and witchcraft, included on some R.E. syllabuses? And spiritualism offers the fascinating prospect of forbidden knowledge about the dead, about the future, about life after death.

As they reach adolescence children develop an increased ability to think symbolically. It is characteristic of youth to use this ability to daydream and to meditate, principally about love and about death. Although sexual and social maturity bring the much desired independence within sight, they do not necessarily bring self-confidence. The speed of physical change can be unnerving, boy/girl relationships bring their problems and embarrassments, and emotions are liable to swing dramatically from the crest of the wave to the depths of despair.

Adolescents may appear brash and self-opinionated, but beneath that facade they are often very unsure of themselves. They are seeking to know who they really are, and in that search for identity sexuality plays a major part. The current confusion about homosexuality and heterosexuality and the minimising of sex differences is not helpful to the adolescent for it undermines the strong sex role which could underpin his or her self-image. Failure to achieve a satisfactory self-image and sense of worth can contribute towards suicidal tendencies which are not uncommon in adolescence, with its fits of anxiety and depression and sometimes morbid thoughts about death.

Because our advice is often strongly resented it is tempting to opt out of the parental role as our children reach for adult status. But our generation has seen too much of parental abdication and its tragic consequences in terms of drop-outs, suicides and unwanted babies. As parents and teachers we have a great opportunity to help children through this time of turmoil by supporting them through their sometimes bizarre phases of dress and appearance until they find themselves. We must still be there at the end of the day. We can treat with respect their attempts to solve the problems of the world, and the mystery of life and death. We can offer them rational replies to those who regard it as the end of being. This is the time to discover exactly what the Bible does say about death, and to talk through all the other ideas that may have been gathered on the subject. It is reassuring to dispel many mistaken ideas or fears by the light of Scripture.

This chapter has been concerned with the growth of a concept. The next will consider a different sort of perception.

3
Spiritually discerned

Children also develop in their spiritual awareness. Things may be grasped spiritually long before they are understood intellectually. While avoiding language that might create confusing impressions, parents can provide a clear framework in which faith may grow.

Eye hath not seen, nor ear heard, nor hath it entered into the heart of man, what God hath prepared for them that love him. (1 Corinthians 2:9 A.V.) But we know about these things because God has sent his Spirit to tell us . . . But the man who isn't a Christian can't understand and can't accept these thoughts from God, which the Holy Spirit teaches us. They sound foolish to him because only those who have the Holy Spirit within them can understand what the Holy Spirit means. Others just can't take it in. 1 Corinthians 2:10, 14 (The Living Bible)

A child's ideas about death do not develop in isolation. They are bound up with the total growth of understanding, of personality and of spiritual awareness. With or without direct teaching on the subject he is bound, as he grows up, to meet with speculations of various sorts about what follows death. He will accept those that his intelligence, personality and upbringing recommend as true. His thinking about an afterlife will be affected by ideas about God that have been acquired through intellectual channels: but intellectual channels are not the only means by which we grow. There is also access to understanding through the emotions, and there is direct knowledge of God through personal experience.

Not this world's wisdom

The Bible tells us explicitly that there is a type of knowledge that has no direct dependence on those powers of abstract thought which do not develop in full before the age of puberty. It is available to the very young and also to the mentally handicapped. In her touching biography of a retarded child, Melissa, Diana Baumgarten[2] tells of seven-year-old Lori, whose problems included mental handicap, spina bifida and hydrocephalus. 'Did ya know Jesus lives in my heart?' she asked an astonished taxi-driver. 'Yup. And he can live in your heart too.' This type of knowledge is 'not what is called wisdom by this world,' it is 'that mysterious secret wisdom of God.' (1 Corinthians 2:6,7)

Educational theories which cover only the intellectual and emotional aspects of growth in a child's understanding are inadequate. They do not allow for this faculty, which is spiritual. St Paul makes it very clear that this spiritual element is not to be confused with the intellect by which abstract ideas are formulated:

It is these things (i.e. heavenly things) that we talk about, not using the expressions of the human intellect but those which the Holy Spirit teaches us, explaining spiritual things to those who are spiritual. But the unspiritual man simply cannot accept the matters which the Spirit deals with – they just don't make sense to him for, after all, you must be spiritual to see spiritual things. 1 Corinthians 2:14 (J. B. Phillips)

This knowledge, then, is not something that children or adults work out for themselves. It is not accessible through the intellect alone, nor only through the feelings (which would be pure emotionalism), though no doubt God may make use of these channels as well in communicating that which he wishes us to know about himself and about what happens after death.

Spiritual awareness

Every child is born with this many-faceted being, and every child grows up in two environments – the natural and the supernatural. Yet little attention is given to the life of the spirit in our educational system. All the nurturing that the child receives is on the physical side, so his spiritual awareness atrophies. The arts do have a spiritual aspect, and there may be a small spiritual component amidst the sociological, moral and cultural aspects of R.E. – but we really know very little about the spiritual development of children.

Even so, many parents and teachers have been impressed by the spirituality which even very young children have evidenced in their response and in their prayers. They show a grasp of some of the fundamentals of Christian faith, although they might express it in a concrete form and would not be able to handle it conceptually.

Jonathan, aged 5, did not want to stay at school for his dinner. He went to school that morning unhappily resigned to having his dinner there. At the end of the morning he was unexpectedly reprieved by the fact that his father could fetch him home. He expressed his relief in the rapturous words, 'God does LOVE me!'

Two-year-old Nicola, who had been listening to her parents arguing, turned to them and said, 'Praise the Lord all the day,' which dispelled their argument immediately! In his critique of the research and conclusions of Dr R. Goldman, whose theories have had such a far-reaching influence on religious education, Kenneth Howkins[3] examines the idea that children develop through three stages, pre-religious, sub-religious and religious; and that we do not reach the 'religious' stage until adolescence:

> Dr. Goldman is thinking in terms of intellectual concepts and formulations. But many of us can look back to distinctly religious thought and experience long before adolescence. If the basic concepts of Christian orthodoxy – goodness, dependence, trust, obedience, responsibility, guilt, punishment, forgiveness, trustworthiness, love – are part of children's emotional experience at an early age, then despite inadequate intellectual grasp or inadequate ability to verbalise such experiences, they can truly understand what the Bible's central message is about.

There is no doubt that to Jonathan the intervention of God in saving him from something he dreaded was very real, while Nicola was aware that there was something wrong with arguing that could be put right by a proper attitude of praise. Kenneth Howkins illustrates his point with the story of a six-year-old boy who was chased by a big boy while on his way home from school:

> He was very frightened, and he stopped suddenly in the street, with many people about, put his hands together, and called out aloud, 'Lord, help me!' He then dashed into the nearest shop doorway, and the big boy passed by without seeing him. The next day he gave his testimony to the teacher: 'I spok (sic) to God last night.'

> That incident is worth further consideration. First, that the child understood something about religion. I doubt if he could state much about his ideas on prayer, or the methods of divine intervention, but his practical action shows his understanding. Dr. Goldman may call this a primitive view of prayer. I do not. For that child it was a major affair, and the answer may be physical not spiritual, but here is the child putting into practice a childlike faith. Is not this the child-like quality which Christ Himself demands?[3]

Some educationists hold that you cannot mention God to infants, on the grounds that they cannot understand abstract concepts. Presumably the same would be said about heaven. In any event it would be meaningless to talk about heaven with no mention of God. But God is not an abstract concept – He is a living person! Kenneth Howkins has made the point with beautiful clarity in an article 'Teaching about the Exodus'[4]

> You, the reader, are a Human Being. That term 'Human Being' is an abstract concept and it is quite difficult to define . . . But you, the reader, are not an abstract concept: you are a man, or a woman, a living person, a human being. Clearly, one way of talking about people is concrete, and another is abstract. Both ways have their place . . . We do not try to introduce to Infants an abstract notion of God, or a theological or philosophical definition. But the story of Moses and the Exodus is a fine, concrete way of talking

about God. The God of the Bible – the whole Bible – is the living God, who acts and speaks.

It was the same God who called the child Samuel, and he still calls children today. He can initiate the relationship and make his presence known to a child, as is shown by the spontaneous trust of their prayers. One little boy, kneeling by his bed, was heard to say, 'Come closer, gentle Jesus, I want to whisper this bit.'

Appropriate language

The following record from a Christian family is interesting in that it shows how the literal thinking of a young child can develop into the full intellectual and spiritual awareness of a Christ-filled personality:

David, now aged 4 years:

Q: Who is Jesus?
David: A boy like me. He was a baby when he was born.
Q: What happened to Jesus?
David: He died on a cross for me. He came alive again.
Q: Where is Jesus now?
David: In heaven. You can talk to him. He knows all about you 'cause he's Christ. He's in my tummy. If you die you can go to Jesus. He knows my name. When cowboys die do they go to Jesus?

Christopher, aged 6 years:

Q: What do you think about Jesus?
Christopher: He's in heaven. He loves everybody, he cares for everybody and he made everybody. Sometimes he gives me a feeling that he's there and loves me. It makes me feel happy.
Q: What happened at Canterbury Christian Camp last summer?
Christopher: I gave my life to the Lord. That made me very happy and I know that he cares for me.

The parent writes of Christopher's spiritual experience: 'He was given a Good News Bible then and has read it from then on as best he can. It was a very real experience at the time. He was aglow. He was 6¼ years then. When he was younger he used to speak of Jesus being in his tummy and ask if there was enough room for Jesus when he had eaten his dinner!'

Karen, now 11½ years:

> She used to think of Jesus as 'a powerful big man. He could do miracles and magic like he could take ghosts away. She knew him to talk to. She would ask him to give her a good day and make her better when she was ill. She thought of him as sitting on a big throne in space. He was with her because he had the whole world in his big hands and she was walking in his hands.'

Nicola, now 13 years, cannot really remember what she thought when she was only 4 or 5 years old, but God has always been real to her.

A lady wrote, 'My friend's little boy, aged 6 years, speaks of God as being in his head and naturally talks to him to make him better when he is unwell.' Jonathan, at the age of five, told me, 'I'm a Christian. I asked Jesus into my heart yesterday.' This experience meant a great deal to him at the time, and a year later is still an enduring reality in his thinking and in his life.

These children have expressed their perception of Christ's presence in the literal image of 'head' and 'heart' and 'tummy', in a way that is appropriate to their years, but this has not hindered their spiritual development. The 'concrete' terms represent a real experience, and gradually the thinking is modified as the years advance, but the reality remains. However, these are children who have sound Christian nurturing, and there are other ways of speaking about the real presence of Jesus that may be more helpful to children who do not have that advantage, e.g. 'Jesus is with you' or 'Saying "yes"' to Jesus. The fact that children think in literal terms is no hindrance to their talking about spiritual things, among which we may include life after death. But it is always important to bear in mind what the child's upbringing and home may be, whether Christian or not, and to consider what the words we choose may convey to them in the light of their previous language experience.

Recently I was told of a middle-aged lady who was shown a

reproduction of Holman Hunt's painting 'The Light of the World', when she was a child. She had asked what it was about – what it meant. She was told that it was a picture of the Lord Jesus Christ knocking at the door of the human heart and asking to be taken in. She was so impressed by this visual representation of spiritual truth that she straightway asked the Lord into her heart.

This was a life-transforming experience which she could look back upon from the perspective of maturity and know to have been genuine and lasting. The literal representation had worked upon her childish imagination as a medium of grace. That is how symbolism works.

Similarly, some of the imagery of the now unfashionable old children's hymns may help them to think about things that would otherwise be beyond them, e.g. 'There's a home for little children above the bright blue sky,' where the word 'home' carries associations of comfort and security.

Although children cannot handle abstract reasoning as adults do, we must remember: (i) that spiritual truths (Jesus loves me) are not to be confused with abstract ideas (Beauty is truth). Abstract ideas have their existence in the human mind; spiritual truths have an independent reality whether we are thinking about them or not. Spiritual truths may be experienced, though perhaps not understood. In this case the example of an abstract idea, 'Beauty is truth', *is* outside the child's experience. But the example of a spiritual truth, 'Jesus loves me', is within the child's experience, being centred on the word 'love'. Love *is* abstract, but it is, at least to an extent, within the child's experience. In fact, all three words (Jesus loves me) have a meaning for the child, whereas all three words (Beauty is truth), are very remote individually, and more so when put together.

> A weaver who finds hard words in his hymnbook knows nothing of abstractions – just as a child knows nothing of maternal love, but only knows one face and one lap to which it turns for nurture and for comfort.
> (George Eliot, in *Silas Marner*.)

So a child who doesn't know the words can yet experience the love of Christ.

(ii) that children of infant school age can understand some

abstract concepts, without being able to manipulate them in an abstract way:

> Stories about men and women doing things are concrete enough. We can have exciting, concrete stories about brave and courageous exploits, and infants love the stories. We can easily go on from the story and talk about the courage of the hero, or other virtues or failings. So we find ourselves talking about something abstract – even with infants . . .

> Infants do have the notions of 'brave' or 'kind', or 'good', or 'strong'. Of course, the notion gradually becomes more refined, but the notion, with some real content, is there, in infants.   *Religious Studies Today*[4]

(iii) that

> the distinction between abstract and concrete ideas is by no means so clean-cut as some people imagine. In fact an abstract idea can be 'abstracted' from a lot of concrete objects. That is how the infant mind learns to speak.

> So we have two warnings: do not wrongly define 'abstract', and do not underestimate the infant mind.
>   *Religious Studies Today*[4]

When exploring the idea of death with children we need to be aware of the complexity of the whole situation, the different possibilities that words may hold, the feelings that are involved. An example of truly abstract thinking that involved death can be found in the following: on 1st February Jonathan (6) wrote in his school diary, 'I love Mummy. I love Daddy. I love Peter. Space is eternal. I feel sad.' Asked what he meant, he replied, 'Space goes on and on for ever. But we don't. We will die.'

When his parents saw the diary they were able to explain that we too will 'go on and on forever' in heaven with the Lord. Children do not all develop at the same rate, and this is true not only of physical and intellectual growth but also of the spiritual faculty we have been considering. Much depends on the environment in which they have been brought up, if they have sensed Christ's presence in their family prayer times or in church worship. The questions they ask about spiritual matters may well be among the most difficult ones we have to answer, especially as it is not always easy to know just what lies behind a child's questions. We need to listen sensitively and to 'read between the lines', as it were. A golden rule is never to pre-empt the question, never to answer more than the child is ready for. One mother found that the idea of death was too much for her child to take. She had always held firm ideas about the need to answer children's questions honestly. One day her five-year-old told her some story about what his dog would do when he (her son) was a man. She explained gratuitously that the dog would be dead by then. The little boy then asked a question about his own death, which she answered equally honestly. 'The effect was devastating. He went deathly pale, shook with terror and went quite speechless for hours.' The sad fact was that the little boy had originally needed no response to his story beyond her interest.

A child who asks, 'Mummy, what will happen when you die?' for example, may not be thinking about heaven at all but may simply be seeking reassurance that there will be someone to look after him, or that she has no thought of dying for a very long time. The best answers may sometimes be physical – a good cuddle and holding tight – to assure him that you are all going to live for a long, long time.

On the other hand there are children who wonder about death and what it may be like from their early years. Jonathan, at the age of five climbed into his parents' bed one morning and spoke seriously to his father. 'Daddy,' he said, 'one day we will have to part. But then we will be together again for ever.'

Alison (6) and Andrew (5) brought thoughts of heaven and thoughts of God naturally into their conversation about death. Alison thought that, 'Some people die because God needs their help', and, 'Anyway God would be kind to him if he went up there to heaven.' She said that, 'When people die they go up to heaven' and this appeared to be a very satisfactory arrangement as far as she was concerned. Andrew's ideas were less straightforward: 'Sometimes we go up to heaven, and sometimes we just die where we are,' he said enigmatically. The physical and spiritual aspects of death were inextricably bound up together for him: 'Maybe they just probably die there' (i.e. where they are).

He added:

Sometimes there's the crumpled bones left, because I found a sheep's skull and probably it fell off a high cliff into the sea and the bones probably landed on the beaches and the sheep probably died there . . .

But maybe when we got to heaven we'd find the crumpled bones (of a person who had died).

Obviously the finding of the sheep's skull had made a great impression on him and had served to bind his thoughts about heaven to a concrete image. We must expect our children to produce some strange and mistaken ideas about death, but they should not be laughed at as quaint or dismissed as silly. It may be that the difficulty lies, not in the idea, but in the child's ability to verbalise it. Our job is to listen and to explain as simply as possible what we believe.

Ideas about man, his origin and his destiny, have occupied some of the best brains in the history of the world. Bishop Riley has pointed out that 'the problem of death is inseparably bound up with the problems of the nature and purpose of life'.[5] It is also bound up with the problem of evil and of suffering. Sometimes a child's apparently naive question may hold deep philosophical implications:

Another Jonathan, a sensitive 'whimsical' child of average intelligence, the eldest of three in a Christian family, puzzled his parents with the query, made during family prayers when he was five years old: 'Can we pray for the Devil, that Jesus will make him good?'

In a child's terms this poses the age-old question of why a loving God should allow so much licence to the Devil. Sometimes they may be expressing some dimly comprehended truth, in their childish way. The same boy, at the age of seven, after the death of his Great-Grandma, made a request, again during family prayers:

'Daddy, can we pray for Great-Grandma, that she will have a happy funeral and everyone will enjoy it?'

Although at the age of seven he would have a concept of biological death as final, a child of this age believes that identity, his own being, is not limited by time, and as far as

Jonathan was concerned, Great-Grandma had not ceased to be.

It is important not to tell children something that at some later date we shall have to retract. For example it would not only be wrong, it would be silly to tell a child that people go to heaven when they have been good. A sensible child would see this as a reason for being naughty for as long as possible! A simple reply could be, 'We go to heaven because Jesus has made a lovely home there for us when we die.' My sister-in-law began teaching her children while they were very young that, 'Now we live in our body home, but one day when we die we will go to live in our heaven-home.' Although this is a simplification and perhaps not a full representation of biblical truth, it is within a child's comprehension and proved helpful at the time. I also think it would be wiser not to suggest that, 'We go to heaven if we love Jesus', for it suggests the possibility of *not* loving Jesus. That Jesus loves us and that we love him should be mentioned as naturally as 'Daddy and Mummy love you,' and, 'We love them'. It was C. S. Lewis who pointed out that those things are taught most effectively that are assumed to be true, rather than those that are so laboured that they imply that a doubt is possible.

Some people tell children that when we die we become angels and fly about with wings, but in fact angels are a separate form of creation. The Bible teaches that they are God's messengers, not the souls of the departed.

Spiritual Perception

While we should bear in mind when talking to children the fact that their minds do operate somewhat differently from adults', we should not underestimate the capacity of even a two-year-old to have some perception of the reality of the world of the spirit. Young children think literally, they do not think abstractly: but it would be wrong to deduce from this idea that we should postpone talk about God and heaven until they have formed some concept of biological death. On the contrary it is important that they should have a framework of belief about God, about his love for them and about heaven, into which their concept of death may fit at a time and in a manner that is appropriate to the individual child.

4

A framework of belief

It is important to provide children with a framework of belief early in life, into which their thinking about death may fit. The teaching of the Bible about the love and faithfulness of God, the spiritual nature of humankind and the reality of heaven should help them to avoid seeing death as punishment, and to be reassured about life after death and the hope of reunion.

Since we, God's children, are human beings – made of flesh and blood – he became flesh and blood too by being born in human form; for only as a human being could he die and in dying break the power of the devil who had the power of death.

Hebrews 2:14 (The Living Bible).

'The first task of parents is to survive,' commented Derek Nuttall, Director of CRUSE. Since cancer, aeroplane disaster and road accidents take their toll, regardless of human effort or desire, it seemed a strange remark. But the point he was making was the supreme importance of the role of parents in fulfilling the basic needs of children, first and foremost their need to be loved and valued.

However, disasters do happen , and no parent can guarantee to fulfil that first task of surviving. The love we give our children helps to build their early foundation of security, but

51

we are only flesh and blood. We must give them another source of security which will not fail, even if by accident or illness they suffer a parental loss. We must teach them from their earliest years that they are precious not only to us, but also to their Father in heaven, the God who never changes, who does not die, and who says, 'I have loved you with an everlasting love' and, 'I will never leave you nor forsake you.'

We cannot 'programme' for bereavement, but we can help children to develop an inner strength with which to meet all the thousand natural shocks that flesh is heir to – bereavement and death itself among them.

It is here that the framework of Christian belief becomes so important. Although nothing allays the human pain, yet the knowledge that God's love never fails and that nothing can separate us from it, can be a help even to a little child. Kristie's daddy died when she was three years three months. Her mother wrote, '*she* has helped *me* with *her* simple faith.' We do not start from the perspective of death. We start from the perspective of God's love.

God's love and faithfulness

We call God our Father. He so loved us that he sent his only son, Jesus Christ. He knows what it is like to be a human being, to love, to be heartbroken and distressed. He knows what it is like to be a child – 'He was little, weak and helpless, tears and smiles like us he knew.'

It is sadly true that all children do not have good fathers, nor all good mothers, for that matter, and all parents get cross or impatient at times, so we do not teach them that 'God is like your father'. We teach them what God is like, and that they may call him 'Father'. We build their self-esteem and security on the knowledge that he loves them with a changeless and enduring love.

We teach them what 'Father' really means: that he is their protector, their provider; and that he only acts for our good. A child who has a true understanding that God does not act in spite, jealousy or irrational anger should be in a better position to avoid the mistake of thinking 'God took my mummy away because I was so naughty' or 'God loved my brother so much that he took him away from us, to be with him in heaven.'

One of the major anxieties that may trouble a child is what is going to happen to him if daddy, who is the breadwinner, has died. He needs to know that he has a Father in heaven who knows of his plight and who is powerful on his behalf: 'my Father owns the cattle on a thousand hills.'

Our Father listens

We must be careful not to give children the idea that Christians never meet with sorrow and suffering. There is no escapism in the strong faith that looks through death. But even small children are able to find real comfort and strength in the knowledge that God is ready to listen to their prayers. Children who are brought up with saying Grace at mealtimes and simple Goodnight prayers find prayer natural. From the age of three Jonathan would add the names of people he knew to the ones his mother had mentioned. When he was four I was walking with him as he rode his tricycle through the woods. His father was away and for some reason he felt anxious about him. He jumped off his tricycle and stood with his head bowed. 'Let's pray for Daddy,' he said.

But prayers should not be made a chore for reluctant children. If they seem to be treating them as a nuisance or a joke it is better to drop them for a while. Children go through all sorts of phases, and no doubt the God who created them understands the wayward sense of humour and rebellious feelings of a child who is trying to establish the frontiers of his autonomy.

Our Father forgives

Sometimes God is made into a sort of Bogeyman, in much the same way as earthly fathers are used to threaten children into obedience. 'If you don't behave yourself,' some mothers will say, 'I'll tell your father.' Paul Tournier tells of a man who never knew what his father was really like until he went on a journey with him as an adult and found a friend in him. As a child he had been unable to form a relationship with him, because his mother had constantly made him afraid that his father would punish him for every small offence.

It is equally misguided to threaten, 'God won't love you if you're naughty' or, 'If you do that God won't let you go to heaven.' This is so wrong. In the first place it is not true. If entry to heaven depended on goodness none of us would get there. It gives a false picture of God; and it puts a wrong sort of pressure on the child, making heaven into a reward for good behaviour.

Children need to know that their Father in heaven is ready to forgive them when they have been naughty, and that they can approach him in confidence. While it can be harmful to exert such heavy-handed authority that a child is fearful of parental punishment, it is equally unhelpful to overlook wrongdoing. Children know perfectly well that they are not always good and have an inbuilt inclination to go their own way. Andrew, a six-year-old whose father was in training for the ministry, had doubtless taken in some phrases from the Anglican liturgy, for he confessed in his 'Sorry' prayers that one particular misdemeanour was 'his own deliberate fault!' It is healthy for a child to recognise his own failings and to realise that they can be forgiven. This is of great importance for the bereaved child who is blaming himself for the death of a parent or sibling. Such guilt feelings, although unfounded, are very common, and can lead to problems in adult life unless they are talked through and resolved.

A stable faith – built on human images of God

Children's relationships with their parents and with other trustworthy adults make a significant contribution to their developing spirituality, and this will affect both their awareness of God and their understanding of death. The only totally reliable factor in this world is the unchangeableness of God, his love and his justice. These need to be expressed in the human beings who have the care of children in home, school and Sunday School. As children see in our behaviour the steadfastness and consistency that are characteristic of God, so the lessons of Church and Sunday School are reinforced. In this way we

> hold before the growing person the concept of God, all-wise and all-knowing, Who knows the strengths and weaknesses of His human child, and in the doing of Whose will there may be achieved the only truly satisfying integration of the personality.[6]

Through the experiences of childhood the faith and philosophy of the adult are fashioned. In that adult life the man or woman must meet the various frustrations, disappointments and sorrows which life brings. The briefness of life so often cheats us of our ambitions (God said to him, 'Fool! Tonight you die. Then who will get it all?') and the inevitability of its ending sentences us to parting with those we hold dear. But a strong faith can be built in childhood, and can bestow a stability that neither death nor calamity has the power to shake.

The spiritual nature of humankind

Besides knowing something about their Father, children need to know something about themselves. Each of us gradually becomes aware of his or her own individuality as distinct from other members of the family and then from friends. A child may have fair hair like mummy and be tall like daddy, with freckles or dimples like Jimmy or Beth, and the combination is unique. But there is more to the real 'me' than can be seen in the mirror: the knees that get scraped are only one aspect of the real 'me'. Children need to be made aware that God breathed a spirit into their handful of dust. Consciousness of his total being will help a child to realise that he will never cease to be.

Children have a natural empathy with the world of nature. And we encourage this because children can learn so much about God from the world that he has made for us. Dazzling white snow, birds feeding their young, the great expanse of rolling waves, all carry messages about their Creator in a store of mental imagery. Power and purity, beauty and caring are expressed in such pictures. Gerard Manley Hopkins said of the bluebell in his hand, 'I know the beauty of our Lord by it.'

Because they find so much sensory pleasure in nature, and delight, for example, in the squidginess of sand and the splashiness of puddles, children tend to anthropomorphise their findings and to ascribe life to stones and shells.

Frances Hodgson Burnett wrote of her childhood among the forests and mountains that she 'seemed part of the forests themselves', and of the mountains, 'with these too she had that instinct of kinship, of somehow being part of their purple, their clear, dark outline, their dips and curves against the sky.'

More than the earth

But however lovely and uplifting and right in its own way this feeling may be, it is not the whole story. There are two very important truths that we should share.

First, a child should not be left ignorant of the fact that God created him to be more than material.

Great, wide, beautiful, wonderful world,
With the wonderful water round you curled
And the wonderful grass upon your breast –
World, you are beautifully dressed . . .

Ah! you are so great, and I am so small,
I tremble to think of you, World, at all;

And yet, when I said my prayers today,
A whisper inside me seemed to say,
'You are more than the Earth, though you are such a dot:
You can love and think, and the Earth cannot!'
        (William Brighty Rands in *The Book of a Thousand Poems*) (OUP)

The Reality of Heaven

The second truth which could be talked through with an older child is that the spiritual world that lies beyond our sight is no less real than the world of the senses. In fact the letter to the Hebrews states that it is more real. For example, the High Priest used to enter the most holy place of the temple once every year. This was but a shadow: the reality was Christ. He, the real High Priest, entered into heaven itself once for all: . . . the real things in heaven, of which these down here are copies, were made pure with far more precious offerings.

For Christ has entered into heaven itself, to appear now before God as our Friend. It was not in the earthly place of worship that he did this, for that was merely a copy of the real temple in heaven. (Hebrews 9:23/24)

C. S. Lewis expressed this shadow/reality idea in his children's story, *The Last Battle*, where Aslan reveals to the children who have been killed in a railway accident, that they are now in the real world, having left the Shadowlands of mortality behind:

'Our world, England and all, is only a shadow or copy of something in Aslan's real world.' (C. S. Lewis in *The Last Battle*) (Bles/Collins)

Small children, for whom death has no real meaning, may well think of heaven as a place with a geographical location:

'I took the children in my arms and told them that Daddy
had gone to live with Jesus in heaven . . . Later she told me
that she thought heaven was a country overseas.'

However, as she grew up, heaven, as a central part of Rachel's
Christian belief, developed and deepened. Children have
incomplete ideas about many things as they explore; it does not
mean that the subject should be avoided.

The first time my daughter Zoe (then 2 years 4 months) and
I talked about death was when my husband, a Methodist
minister, was out taking a funeral.
From our conversation it was obvious that, up until then,
Zoe had an understanding that death is something to be sad
about.
After asking where Daddy was, and my replying that he'd
gone to a funeral because a lady had died, she said, 'What a
shame.'
I went on to explain that when we love Jesus, and we die, we
come back into life again and live with Jesus. Zoe got the
idea that this was good because she excitedly said, 'and
we'll be happy, won't we?'
    She then went on to explore the idea that each one of us
would die – but was concerned that we shouldn't die just
yet. She understood that we would be together when we
'come back to life again'.
Since then we've talked quite naturally about 'our new
house' i.e. our heavenly mansion. Zoe has asked if she
could take various things with her: I've explained that Jesus
will give us all we need when we get there. She was a bit
upset about not being able to take her teddy – so I didn't
push that one!
Just the other day at three and a half years, Zoe said, quite
out of the blue, 'Because we believe in Jesus, we'll come
back into life again, won't we, and we'll come back into life
again when Jesus says so, won't we?'
Then the next day, 'I won't need my small clothes when I
come back into life again' and, 'We won't come back to our
house, will we?'
I really do thank God that we've conveyed a hopeful
conviction to our daughter, and that she can talk about
'coming back into life again' without any fear. Zoe has

grown up to all three and a half years with Jesus as a much loved and much talked about family friend.

Here are some further conversations on the same subject:

My children have not had to cope with bereavement but my second child, Justin, has always been fascinated by heaven. At four years of age he loved having little bits of Revelation, chapters 21 and 22 read to him, and looked forward to going to heaven to be with the Lord Jesus.

When he was six years old I was one day giving Justin a good talking to because he never looked for traffic when crossing the road. He replied, 'Mummy, I don't know why you're going on at me, because if I get run over I'll be with the Lord Jesus so I'll be happy, and you'll know I am, so you won't have to worry.'

We were talking recently about my 82-year-old father when one of the children said she couldn't bear to think of Grandpa dying soon. 'Well,' said the seven-year-old, 'We wouldn't have to be sad for long because we could look forward to seeing him again in heaven.'

A similar attitude of assurance was shown by Jonathan who was five years four months when his beloved Great-Uncle Ted died. Jonathan went to the funeral and listened intently to the words of the minister. Afterwards Jonathan told his aunt, 'That man said we had lost Uncle Ted, but I don't think he's right because he has gone up to heaven to be with Jesus and one day we'll go up there to be with him.'

Although children learn a great deal from what we actually say, they also catch much from our attitude and the way we say it. Talk about death and dying should not be evasive nor in hushed tones, but positive, natural, hopeful.

When people die children may hear the old platitudes – 'It's the will of God' or 'God's will be done.' This may not be helpful. We should not imply that God meant death and suffering to be part of his plan for his children. Everything we tell them should help them to gain a Biblical concept of the nature of God as loving and caring, as unchanging and worthy of trust, a rock of security.

There are many Bible stories that will help them, of course.

In particular we should tell them how it was that death came into the world. This can be made very simple.

How death came into the world

Long, long ago God made the world, and he made everything in it perfect. He made lions and lambs and trees and stars and butterflies, and everything was healthy and happy. There was no blight on the roses, and nothing died.

God was pleased with the beautiful place he had made.

Then he made a man – Adam – and a woman – Eve – to live in the beautiful place and to look after it, and to be his friends. He told them that everything was theirs to enjoy. But he warned them, 'Don't eat the fruit of the tree that grows in the middle of my beautiful place, for if you do you will die.'

Adam and Eve did as God told them. They looked after the plants and animals, and in the evenings they spent time with God. But one day the serpent came and spoke with Eve. He made her curious about the fruit, and he made her wonder if it was really true that she would die if she ate it. In the end both she and Adam disobeyed God and ate some of the fruit.

God's beautiful place was spoilt, and nothing was ever the same again. It was no longer perfect, and from that time until now every person and every animal and every plant eventually dies. It was not what God had wanted for his world: it was because the man and woman had been disobedient. They had brought sin and suffering into the world and they could no longer be God's friends as they had been. Something had come between them. They had to leave the beautiful place. They had brought death into the world, and one day we too will die.

But God did not leave things like that. He loves us so much that he wants us to live again. He made a plan so that we can be his friends and share his perfect place again. He sent his son, Jesus, to live on this earth, just like one of us, except that Jesus never did any of the wrong things we do. He trusted God and did not doubt what he had said as Adam and Eve had done. He did everything that God wanted him to do. And he died to make up for the disobedience of the first man and woman, and for the wrong things that we do.

When someone dies we bury their body in the ground. But people are not only bodies; they are not simply flesh and bones. The person who is you yourself, like no one else in the world, goes to heaven to be with Jesus in the perfect place. When he was dying on the cross Jesus told the thief who was on the cross beside him that when he died he would go to heaven to be with Jesus.

And everything in heaven is beautiful – just as beautiful as it was when God first made the world. One day God will put right all the things that have gone wrong since Adam and Eve disobeyed him. He will make a new heaven and a new earth. We shall see Jesus there, and we shall even be like him, for we will be beautiful too. All the people we love will be there, and we shall never have to part from them again.

Jesus has gone to make a place ready for us in heaven. He told his friends before he died that they need not be sad or worried, for one day he would come back and take them to heaven with him. He will do the same for us. Heaven is so beautiful that we really cannot imagine just what it will be like. We can think of all the most beautiful things we know here on earth and know that they will be even more beautiful there, for they will be perfect. We do know, too, that it is a very happy place. Nobody there cries or quarrels or is ill. We just are happy there, with Jesus and with all our friends, working and playing and loving one another for ever and ever and ever.

'Mummy,' said Jonathan (nearly five years old) 'I'm worried about Peter. He hasn't asked Jesus into his heart yet, so what will happen to him if he dies? Will he go to heaven?' Since Peter was not yet two we may perhaps smile at the earnestness of his brother. But it is a question asked by adults.

There are two positions regarding what may happen to children who die while they are too young to have made a personal decision for Christ. It is certainly true that children are capable of doing so at an early age, and children whose names appear in this book bear witness to the fact. However, not all children have the opportunity or spiritual understanding to do so. What is their position?

Some people believe that all children are born into a fallen race and therefore have no place in the Kingdom of God until they have made such a commitment. Others believe that children belong to Jesus until they consciously reject him. John Inchley's excellent book *All About Children*[7] argues their case. The two positions are clearly put in Ron Buckland's *Children of the King*:[8]

John Inchley's basic position is that 'all children are included in the great atoning sacrifice, and belong to Jesus Christ until they deliberately refuse Him. David Kingdom's position about the children of Christian *believers* is that they 'are born into the Adamic race and we dare not presume that they have been regenerated until they give real evidence of the saving change,' . . . Kingdon argues that conscious faith (however simple) from the child is the only basis for a relationship with God, and is agnostic about the status of all children prior to the ability to respond with a conscious decision. Inchley on the other hand is saying that all children 'belong to God' until they deliberately refuse him, i.e. exercise conscious acceptance or rejection of God.

Both positions have been argued from Scripture, so parents will have to make a personal decision about which they believe to be true, and will have to answer their children's questions in the light of that belief. We can always say, 'We do not know the answer but we do know that Jesus has a special love for little children. He will do what is best for them.'

5
Preliminary Experiences

There are also practical ways of helping children to come to terms with the idea of death and to cope with bereavement. Among them are providing a stable background; building on experiences of separation; encouraging the habit of free discussion of all their concerns, and learning from pets, nature and books.

Here have we no continuing city, but we seek one that is to come. Hebrews 13:14 (A.V.)

The learning of children is built on past experience, and in this respect learning about death is no different from any other learning. The child's mature response to the idea of death and also to bereavement will be conditioned by the way in which he has been encouraged to think about his world.

A safe place to live in
Talking to children about death as part of their learning about life is very different from talking with a child who has lost a well loved person. In such a situation words may be meaningless and the best help may have been given years before.

The importance of a sense of security has been mentioned, but as this is a key factor in equipping a child for whatever life or death may bring, something more is due about the way in which this may be developed or shaken.

Has his experience included fear, loneliness and anxiety, for instance, or has it taught him that the world is a safe place to live in: that changes do come, but that they are not always for the worse, that love surrounds him?

From the very beginning his environment speaks eloquently to the child about what he may expect from life, and this will mould his thinking about death and his response to losing a loved one. A child left to cry for a long time can frighten himself by his own crying and become hysterical. It is always best to check nothing is amiss, or simply to reassure. Light sleepers can do with a glow lamp; and this does away with the constant putting on of the bedroom light when you go in, which teaches a child to associate light with companionship, and darkness with being alone and afraid. He needs to learn that dark and light are both alike in harbouring no terrors.

A toddler should not be torn from his mother's arms by some well-meaning baby-sitter, trying to help her to get out on time. A less traumatic parting should be planned. Toddlers should develop their independence by small absences before there is a long or sudden parting. All small children go through a stage when they need their mother in sight, but it does not last long.

The transition from home to school is a big step which nursery school may help to bridge. However, some mothers may prefer to have their children at home; and play-groups or mums-and-toddlers offer the chance for them to socialise together. Whichever choice is made, love is the key factor – security flows from love. Even in a very poor home children can gain as much stimulation as they need, tumbling about in the kitchen, and chattering to mummy about their activities with water and dough and objects of various shapes and sizes, or helping her cook and clean. Some partings cannot be avoided – serious illness, for example, may mean hospitalisation, but many hospitals now make arrangements for parents to stay close at hand and help with feeding their children, recognising that this may speed their recovery. It does not matter if the environment changes, provided the parents are around. They are the child's greatest source of security, and in making a happy home with loving relationships, they are building a good foundation for the child's developing personality.

Provide security, and then the child can deal with loss.

Feigned deaths

> But since that I
> Must die at last, 'tis best,
> To use myself in jest
> Thus by feigned deaths to die.

A child who knows that his home base is secure can launch out into gradually lengthening absences from it. He sees that he does not need to have the love object always within sight, that he can cope on his own. John Donne's words above suggest that we should make better use of our learning material in building on short and temporary partings.

Unhappy, bitter or unprepared experiences of early separation may damage a child, undermining confidence and leading to later depression; and this should be borne in mind when considering sending a child to boarding-school. Many go at the age of seven, which is an age of formation. On the other hand it is through such changes, starting school, changing school, moving house, going on holiday, that we all gradually learn to cope with loss. Much depends on the child's degree of self-confidence and personality traits; also on the amount of preparation there has been in adjustment to previous separation experiences. Parents should talk it through with their child beforehand, not leave him in the dark and pack him off willy-nilly. They should aim at a full understanding of what is involved, working through anticipatory loss and making a mutual decision. It is fear of the unknown that makes starting or changing schools so daunting.

We need to encourage our children to talk about their feelings with regard to all areas of their lives, their activities and relationships. It is not easy to find time for talking in our pressurised twentieth-century lives; but it is important to be there when they get home from school, to listen and understand when friends let them down or they have been in trouble in class. Talking over such things helps them to learn creatively from all aspects of change, loss or unhappiness they may encounter. The conviction that God can make all things work together for good to those who love him can only come from looking back and reflecting. Sometimes our experienced eyes can help them to find this true. We also need to acquire the habit of communication, to learn to walk into the area of painful feelings, and so to make it easy for our children to talk about sad things like broken friendships. Otherwise by the time they reach maturity it is too hard.

Children of happy homes can cope with bereavement better than children of homes where there is perpetual discord. It would be an unusual couple who never had a disagreement, but even a quarrel can produce something positive if the children see their parents seeking each other's and God's forgiveness together. This not only gives them a model for behaviour in their own relationships, but it also demonstrates the strength of the framework of a love that holds and it gives them a powerful visual aid of God's forgiveness which could help them to offload any guilty feelings that came to them as a result of a bereavement at some later date.

Treasure on earth

Much of what children will learn about death from their everyday experience will be purely biological, so we must help them to be aware that there are other less tangible aspects of human experience which are just as real as the ground beneath our feet. The spirit of the age is against us – material possessions have an altogether disproportionate place in our lives, but we should try to prevent social pressures making our children too attached to them. Even for children they have become status symbols, and it is hard on the toddler who has no pedalcar, or the child without Star Wars galactic fleet toys or computer games, when his friends are boasting.

However, we can emphasise that there are other forms of pleasure. All children have an inherent love of nature which is a wonderful source of joy, and the aesthetic, musical, artistic and creative pleasures open channels to the spiritual world.

'Goodbye, Scamp'

Pets can play a special part in children's emotional development, not least in their encounter with death. Children can chase, cuddle, confide in their dog, and know that the love he gives is not based on anything but unqualified devotion and acceptance. A dog becomes part of the family: 'How could I – mere mother – presume to remove a friend from the bed of a child when the two were curled up for the night?' wrote Anne

Townsend in Family Magazine, and in the same article sociologist Tony Campolo says:

> Animals teach us the risk of love – there is the risk of loss. If you can't pay the price of sorrow as loss you'll never experience the joy of love. I believe that pets teach us that in spite of the grief of loss it is worth it – and that says something very important in the handling of human relationships. Learning to handle the death of a pet helps children learn to cope with bereavement due to the death of human friend or relation. It is a lesson for life never forgotten.

Children should be allowed to conduct what is an appropriate funeral for a dead pet according to their own ideas – even for a goldfish. They have a basic primitive desire for fitting ritual, and this is an important building opportunity. The woman who threw her child's dead canary in the dustbin, in full view of the child, did violence to her daughter's feelings.

Children very often ask if their pet has gone to heaven, and Christians who have had to answer this question have found it a problem. I can find nothing in the Bible to tell us that there are animals in heaven – but on the other hand I can find nothing to say that there are not. It is a sound educational principle that one should not teach a child something that she will later have to unlearn; but this is a question which cannot be answered definitively even later. Moreover it is an equally sound principle that you should not crush a child with despair. To lose a pet can be a first real sorrow, and a flat harsh denial could be harmful. Perhaps we could say, 'We do not really know the answer, but some people believe that there is a place for animals too.'

Death in the classroom

Keeping small animals in the classroom is one of the ways in which schools can teach a wide variety of important lessons – factual lessons about biology and reproduction, moral lessons about responsibility and kindness – and among them the inevitability and finality of death.

Sex education is now an integral part of our children's schooling, even though many are not happy about the way in which little place may be given to the moral and spiritual aspects of the subject. People feel even more dubious about any kind of 'death education', although the need to break the taboo is widely recognised. One correspondent wrote:

> As a teacher, I feel one would have to tread very warily in dealing with the topic in a formal classroom setting. There are so many obvious pitfalls. (a) Are you sure that none of the children in the class has suffered traumatic bereavement – if they have, a generalised class discussion might be the worst thing for them? (b) Most classes are multi-racial – parents of other faiths would not welcome a specifically Christian approach to bereavement, and it might confuse children dangerously. For older, secondary children one could look at various approaches to belief in an afterlife – but surely again this must be a comparative study. I asked my daughter what she thought about 'death' as a classroom topic. 'Oh no, that would be horrible. All the boys would get gory and tell awful stories and the girls would either cry or get the giggles 'cause they were embarrassed.'

The need for sensitivity concerning individual children does, of course, apply to many situations, and teachers who handle creative writing are as likely to be alert to this as Religious Education specialists will be aware of the desirability of exploring the approaches of other faiths. Nonetheless it may well prove helpful to offer some opportunity of acquaintance with an area which has hitherto been shunned – not in the form of a one-off lesson or project, but as an awareness apparent in the course of different parts of the curriculum, at different stages of schooling. Any such exploration must bear in mind that the children's understanding develops in stages, passing through the ability to distinguish between living, dead and inanimate objects to the realisation that death happens to human beings; and finally to the knowledge that this will happen to their loved ones and themselves.

Much can be done as it arises in connection with the classroom pets, the nature table and the seasonal changes, the categorising of objects as alive, dead or never alive, with talk about what this means; while a study of the life-cycle of the dragonfly and its adaptation for each stage of life in a different dimension, would supply the children with an analogy for

67

physical and spiritual life which could be enlightened at some future time.

A study might be made of different artists' interpretations of death; and in dance and drama seasonal themes might be explored, and the expression of grief, joy, resurrection etc. through music or movement.

Picture language

Children can be helped to come to terms with the idea of death by seeing it in the context of life and of nature: a new spiritual life in a new dimension can be so realistically pictured in the plant which springs miraculously from a little dry seed planted in a yoghurt carton; in the blossom appearing on the dry bough, and in the amazing emergence of the beautiful dragon-fly from the larva in the pond mud to the freedom of flight in the sunlit air, for which it would have been totally unprepared in its old body.

In general the language which they meet in school is impoverished of the imagery which would furnish the material for 'otherworldly' thinking. Even in their hymns it became 'with-it' to dismiss those with gates of pearl, white robes and golden crowns, on the grounds that they were not in line with the child's actual experience. Yet such language is in fact a very important part of the child's emotional and imaginative experience – not their world of bricks and mortar. There are familiar types of phrase in poetry and fairy tale where they suggest certain states of happiness and heart's fulfillment; and when met in hymns they make the world of the spirit accessible. This is the language of *Pilgrim's Progress*, with its powerful visual images and stirring appeal to the ear: 'and all the trumpets sounded for him on the other side'. All children should have the opportunity of reading it, for the importance of such imagery and symbolism in conveying ideas about death and the afterlife cannot be overstated. There are no other terms with which we can express the inexpressible than by using the paraphernalia of everyday life. In Milton's words, 'All learning is rooted in the objects of sense'. Through such picture phrases, which a child's mind can grasp, he can begin to learn about the truths they represent before he would be capable of thinking about them in the abstract.

Myths and fantasies about death (C. S. Lewis' Narnia Tales

and George Macdonald's *At the Back of the North Wind*, for instance) operate in the same way:

> Listening to myths and fantasies is an education in thinking in images and symbols, and in thinking about things that cannot be apprehended in any other way.
>
> (Elizabeth Cook in *The Ordinary and The Fabulous*.)

The place of books

'Books also helped' wrote a widowed mother. Indeed, books can help in many ways: the experience of home and school can be extended considerably by the insights gained from them, and they can have a positive role in enlarging a child's understanding of death and in affording comfort to those who have been bereaved.

For a small child the story itself may be of secondary importance to the opportunity it offers for sitting on someone's lap and being cuddled. Turning the pages, looking at the pictures may take him into another world for a while, and this can be a welcome experience for a child who is unable to face the reality of the situation. Older children, too, may find the escapist aspect helpful:

> 'I would read to rid my mind of the horrid thoughts! (*Questionnaire*)

However, although initially fiction may be welcomed as an escape route for the feelings, there is also a place for giving emotions free rein through the various experiences which literature can offer, by means of the imagination.

Victorian writers treated death in association with Heaven, freely and naturally, because their own faith was also the generally held belief of the time. Between the wars society became more secular and more materialistic; while at the same time childhood began to be regarded as a golden time that should be untroubled by the harsh realities of life. Death, together with violence, handicap and all that makes the darker side of life, disappeared from children's stories.

The last decade has seen a significant change. Advances in child psychology have made it apparent that we do children no kindness if we shelter them from all the problems life holds and the end that awaits us.

Many parents believe that only conscious reality or pleasant and wish-fulfilling images should be presented to the child – that he should be exposed to only the sunny side of things. But such one-sided fare nourishes the mind in only a one-sided way. And real life is not all sunny.

> (Bruno Bettelheim in *The Uses of Enchantment: the Meaning and Purpose of Fairy Tales*) (Thames and Hudson)

In any event the coming of television has thrust children into the adult world willynilly, war and death and all.

Books can give them a realistic approach to death, but at their own level; and they can provide a starting point for talking through their experience if they have been bereaved. Stories about children who have suffered a similar experience allow them to view those feelings objectively and make it possible to talk about them. Several publishing firms have brought out books to provide such talking points. Situation books such as *The Day Grandma Died* by Jan Felby (CIO) and *Why Did Grandma Die?* by Trudy Madler (Blackwell-Raintree) provide settings in which a child may talk freely and naturally about what has happened and ask questions as they arise in the context of the story. Like photographs, they may bring back happy memories – and remembering helps.

As we have seen, sorrow is not the only emotion which bereavement produces. Guilt or anger may be tangled up with other negative feelings, and for some younger readers these may be released through the medium of fairy tales. The characters in fairy tale are very clearly drawn: they demonstrate anger or hatred or goodness without the ambivalence of human nature. They present the polarities of human behaviour and are less essentially people than cyphers by which a child can work through his feelings of anger or hatred and yet can still identify with the hero or heroine who surmounts all the difficulties. They suggest that there do exist solutions to the anxieties that the reader is experiencing; and some of them convey spiritual ideas. 'Briar Rose' suggests that love is stronger than death; 'Beauty and the Beast' also speaks of the transforming and revivifying power of love. But this is not true of all fairy tales: some of Grimm's are too horrific, while some modern ones are superficial or vacuous, so you do need to be discerning, both about the story and also about the edition in which it is produced, illustrations as well.

Death appears in many young adult novels now, and teenagers might find that reading about the trauma of youngsters of their own age in their own period setting may help to resolve their inner conflicts.

A Star for the Latecomer, by Paul and Bonnie Zindel, is a sensitive study of the relationship between a teenage girl and her mother who is dying of cancer. Throughout her life the mother has pressurised her talented daughter to follow a stage career, while the daughter's desire is simply to marry a nice boy and make a home of her own. Reluctantly the girl finds herself rebelling against her mother, wanting to hate her, though at the same time she also loves and admires her. The fact that her mother is dying exacerbates the guilt feelings generated by this divisive pull. However, the final influence of much teenage literature may be neither desirable nor positive and it is always wise to know what your children are reading.

Positive pictures of children learning to cope after the death of parents are given in *The Night Swimmers*, by Betsy Byars [The Bodley Head], *I am David*, by Anne Holm [Methuen], *The Good Master*, by Kate Seredy [Harper and Row] and *The Pastures of the Blue Crane* by H. F. Brinsmead [O.U.P.].

Spiritual framework

Death is once again a major theme in children's literature, but there is in general a difference between the stories of today and those of the nineteenth century. While the stories of today do offer realistic treatment of the subject from a biological and psychological point of view, they are silent about what may come after, nor do they offer the ultimate solution for feelings of guilt, the forgiveness which makes free indeed. They omit the spiritual framework which gives meaning to life and to death. The truth of Heaven, the hope of re-union, the affirmation of eternal life, all these made an integral part of the work of Mrs Ewing, George Macdonald, Hans Andersen, A.L.O.E. and many other Victorians whose stories were widely read and influential. In the majority of today's stories the child who looks down at the still face in the coffin sees no pointer to hope.

However, there are some notable exceptions. In *The Brothers Lionheart* [Hodder and Stoughton] for instance,

Astrid Lindgren pictures the human spirit living on in a great adventure 'somewhere on the other side of the stars', and the magnificent ending of *Watership Down*, by Richard Adams [Penguin], mentioned elsewhere as being helpful to a child, proclaims that we continue joyfully into a new existence. Although these are not Christian in their portrayal of the nature of humanity, they are a welcome change from the materialistic view of many current stories which treat of death. In the outworking of her plots Patricia St. John shows the way through to a real healing of mind and soul, and freedom from guilt, anger and grief in the wake of death. Her teenage novel, *Nothing Else Matters* [SU] takes war, death, sorrow and reconciliation as its major themes; and through its vivid portrayal of the fighting in Lebanon shows the true solution to emotional and psychological trauma to lie in the all-embracing love of Christ.

Many children of Christian homes may wonder why their prayers have not been answered in the way they wished. In some of the letters in this book parents have shown how they answered this deep and difficult question. Patricia St John has illustrated her own view in the picture language which is so meaningful to children:

> 'I prayed so hard he would get better,' I said despondently, 'but it didn't do any good. God didn't listen and Terry died.'
>
> 'Little maid,' replied Mr. Tandy rather hesitantly, 'if you come to me and says "There's a little lame lamb down yonder what can't run about" – on account of the pasture being steep like, and the stones sharp – and s'pos'n I comed down and picked up that little lamb and carried him in my arms to another pasture where the grass was sweet and the ground easy-like, you wouldn't come and tell me as I hadn't heeded you, would you now?'
>
> I gazed at him dumbly. I was beginning to understand.
>
> (From *The Tanglewoods' Secret* by Patricia St. John) [Scripture Union]

C. S. Lewis believed that this life is only a shadow of a much more wonderful life to come. We are in one dimension, but there is another dimension around us, a spiritual one, and when we die we go through into that dimension. It becomes real to us. This is very close to what the Bible teaches: that this life is not all that there is for us – death is not the end; that Jesus has gone to prepare a place for us where we can be with him forever, where there will be no more illness, sorrow, parting, death and where we can find again those whom we love here:

> For we know that when this tent we live in – our body here on earth – is finished, God will have a house in heaven for us to live in, a home he himself has made, which will last forever. (2 Corinthians 5:1 Amplified)

The Narnia Chronicles are an education in philosophical concepts through the medium of pictures, 'in thinking about things that cannot be apprehended in any other way'. As we have already seen in chapter 3, C. S. Lewis tells us, through the picture language of his stories, that the land we live in is the unreal one, and that it is only when we pass through the curtain of death that we shall find ourselves in the real one. The following passage extends an idea also quoted from *The Last Battle* in the previous chapter.

> . . . Peter and Edmund and Lucy gasped with amazement and shouted out and began waving: for there they saw their own father and mother, waving back at them across the great, deep valley.
>
> 'How can we get at them?' asked Lucy.
>
> 'That is easy,' said Mr. Tumnus. 'That country and this country – all the real countries – are only spurs jutting out from the great mountains of Aslan. We only have to walk along the ridge, upward and inward, till it all joins up' . . . and across that valley the land which was the real England grew nearer and nearer . . .
>
> 'There was a real railway accident,' said Aslan softly, 'Your father and mother and all of you are – as you used to call it in the Shadowlands – dead. The dream is ended: this is the morning.' (C. S. Lewis in *The Last Battle*)

Children do not always see the significance of the great Lion, Aslan, and they may not take in all that is implied in the Narnia stories at a conscious level. But the imagery remains with them and becomes part of their thinking. Later in life the truth dawns on them, an experience which students have shared with me.

A very straightforward treatment of the subject carries a

message of comfort for younger children in the beautifully produced *Grandpa and Me* by Marlee and Benny Alex (Lion), illustrated by photographs:

> 'The seasons are God's way of telling us that it isn't the end when we die. In winter the leaves fall off the trees, but in spring the new buds bring new leaves. That's like the new life we have with God in heaven.'
> 'What's heaven like?'
> 'Well,' said Grandpa, 'there's no more sadness or illness. God gives us a new body to live in which will never die. It's a lovely place. I shouldn't be too sad.'

6

Mourning and the Growing Child

Children may appear to be unmoved by the death of a parent at the time, but this does not necessarily mean that they have not been deeply affected. It is possible that children do not pass through the same stages of mourning as are recognisable in adults. Some people think that it is not until the separation of adolescence is completed that such a pattern of mourning is possible. The real hurt may show only in adult life.

Love is strong as death . . . many waters cannot quench love. The Song of Solomon 8:6,7 (A.V.)

The price of love

It is love that gives meaning to life, but it involves a cost. The grief we feel when we lose someone dear is the price of that love. We could not be without the love, and we must accept the grief. But it is so much harder when there are children involved, because of their helplessness, and because we feel that childhood should be a time of unclouded happiness. Yet even children must share that cost if there is a death in the family, for a disastrous mistake can be made by trying to hide the truth from them.

The death of a parent means the rending of love ties that have been forming from before birth. Speaking about friends,

Polonius advised Laertes to 'grapple them to thy heart with hoops of steel', but this has already been done for us with our family. We owe much of what we know about 'bonding', or the forming of these attachment ties to Dr John Bowlby, the distinguished paediatrician attached to the Tavistock Clinic. He has shown that the love-bonds which we form in infancy affect the formation of relationships in later years, and that their disruption can have deep and lasting effects.

Our capacity to make strong bonds of affection with other human beings is one of the characteristics by which we show ourselves to be formed in the image of God. It is a spiritual inheritance, but it is rooted deeply in our physical senses of sight and smell and touch. One of my father's memories in the few weeks before he died was of his mother's scent of fresh violets, now taking him back to his childhood. Tennyson's words hit the spot:

> But, O for the touch of a vanished hand
> And the sound of a voice that is still.

The mechanism of bonding relies heavily on the sense of touch – on the baby's enjoyment of her mother's warm body, on the secure strength of a father's arms, on the cuddles and caresses and romps of growing up. These bodily contacts cement the bonds of love.

As soon as a baby becomes sufficiently conscious of his own selfhood to feel attached to another person he begins to know the fear of losing that person. We sometimes hear people say, 'He's tied to his mother's apron strings', or, 'She won't let her mother out of her sight,' or, 'The baby means everything to her', or, 'He lives for that boy of his.' This is the way people recognise the bonds of love. And here are the roots of both the fear of death and the pain of bereavement.

All childhood experiences have critical importance for the future. In *The Mill on the Floss* George Eliot traces the development of Maggie's passionate attachment to her brother, formed in her tempestuous childhood. It is a devotion that dominates her maturing emotions and moulds her womanhood:

> Life did change for Maggie and Tom, but they were not wrong in believing that the thoughts and loves of these first years would always make part of their lives.

Pondering on our childhood experiences she later adds, 'Every one of those keen moments has left its trace and lives in us still.' During the last three decades there has been much research conducted into the disastrous results that can ensue, whether at the time or in later life, from the disruption of the bonds of love in childhood.

Mourning

Bereavement is the death of someone to whom we have been strongly bonded; grief is the expression of the wound sustained, and mourning is nature's way of healing that wound. All peoples and all cultures have their own ways of mourning; wherever there are strong attachments, and where these have been broken, there will be mourning, even among birds and animals as well. Among the mountains of Wales during a particularly hard winter, my neighbour came across the bodies of two birds in the snow. One, still soft, was lying with wings outspread across the frozen body of the other. It had refused to leave its mate.

The tale of Greyfriars Bobby is well known. The little terrier followed the body of the old shepherd, his beloved master, in funeral procession to the graveyard, and refused to leave the grave in spite of all enticements. He lived and died in the shelter of the gravestone, through all the wintry weather, feeding on rats and mice caught among the graves, and scraps brought by friendly folks. Mourning, then, is an expression of grief which we share with many creatures.

But there are differences of opinion as to whether children go through the same process of mourning as adults do. First, there is shock, which may produce a sort of numbness when the mind refuses to take in what has happened. 'I just can't believe it', is a common reaction, and it may sometimes take weeks before the real grieving begins.

This may be expressed in a variety of powerful responses – loud cries, sobbing, weeping or rage. Often people direct their anger against God, questioning his love, his justice and his omnipotence. 'How could a God of love allow this to happen?' or, 'If God is all-powerful why did he let her die?' or, 'It's not fair of God – he was only so young', even Christians will say. Indeed, such questions are relevant only from Christians. For if our lives are simply a matter of chance, anything may happen.

There is only a problem if you believe that God loves us and also that he has everything that happens under his control.

Great Shining Tears

Job's suffering and his questioning stand for all time as a picture of the great mystery which confronts every family which loses a young father in an accident, a young mother of a brain tumour. As Evangelicals we tend to assume that the Bible will spell out specific answers to all our questions. To this question there is no such answer in terms of human rationality, but there is something better.

Scripture gives us the assurance that the tragedy which has hit us so hard does not mean that God's love has been withdrawn. 'When you go through deep waters and great trouble I will be with you.' (Isaiah 43:2, *The Living Bible*) At the same time the mystery is not 'solved' as if this were some puzzle that could be worked out – how dreadful it would be if this were so. How dreadful it would be if there were no place for wonder, for awe in our relationship with the Almighty. How limited we would be if all the intricate workings of this amazing universe, and all the strange secrets of the human soul were laid bare. How insecure we would be with our pygmy god, whose grace would be no more than human morality, whose mercy no more than human kindness. Our brilliant computer-like brains are built for this dimension only, and mystery must always be the veil which hides the Godhead.

Best of all, the Bible makes the tremendous assertion that God actually feels our sorrow and suffers with us. 'In all their affliction he was afflicted' (Isaiah 63:9 *The Living Bible*), and in the Incarnation and at Calvary God identified himself with our human flesh and with our suffering. Jesus wept – but he did not only weep for someone else's pain. He agonised in his own.

This is difficult to tell to a child, but C. S. Lewis, whose tales so often provide a bridge, which even a child can cross, to some spiritual truth, has put into his story *The Magician's Nephew*, a picture of what Calvary means. In this story Digory's mother is very ill and Digory dares to ask Aslan for some magic fruit to restore her to health. He is astounded when Aslan does not even answer him, but as he approaches the Lion to ask again he sees that 'great shining tears stood in the Lion's eyes'. There are many who ask for the magic fruit and wonder why they do not receive it. Yet if they can only discern the great tears that are manifest in the Cross they will find that the cloud of unknowing which tragedy draws across our vision does not hide a chasm of horror but a well of love. That love forever surrounds and will sustain them.

Unfortunately bereavement is a time when some may lose their faith, or their sense of God's presence or find it impossible to pray. Yet others find that even in their questioning they draw near to God, and he draws near to them.

Many people are oppressed by guilt. They are filled with regrets and reproach themselves for things they said and for things they failed to do. They try to shut out memories and then feel more guilty for doing so, in a vicious circle of conflicting emotions.

Some people search irrationally in the kitchen or garden, places where their loved ones used to be, or perhaps may suffer physical symptoms such as insomnia, indigestion or palpitations. Depression and despair may follow.

Eventually the long-awaited recovery will begin and it will be possible to think positively about the future, even though the future will never be the same.

This pattern of mourning constitutes a sort of healing process which enables the bereaved person to recover from the experience. If these normal responses do not occur and the bereaved person appears unaffected it is possible that some emotional or psychological trouble may develop later.

Childhood mourning

There are different opinions about the effects of bereavement on children and research is continuing. Sometimes they appear to be curiously matter-of-fact and unmoved, and then, like adults who show little emotion at the time, they may meet trouble later. Some psychologists think that children do not pass through the same grieving process as adults, that adult mourning involves psychological processes for which the child's mind is not equipped before adolescence. Adolescence is seen as a time when the close bonds with parents are broken in a rending of love-ties similar to bereavement. Until this process of liberation is complete, it may not be possible for the child to mourn in the adult sense.

While the function of adult mourning is to detach gradually

the survivor's hopes and memories from the dead, the child's reaction seems to have a contrary aim of avoiding the full impact of accepting death as final. It would be easy to misunderstand the state of mind of the child who shows little sign of sorrow, throwing himself into school affairs, hobbies and activities with friends, apparently forgetful of the dead parent; but such a child might be denying the reality of his loss with one part of his mind, while conscious of it in another. An intelligent ten-year-old said, 'I know that my father is dead, but what I cannot understand is why he doesn't come home for dinner.'

However, not all children are unmoved and some are affected deeply at the time. Seven-year-old Ruth, who attended the same dancing-class as I, belonged to a very close family of four – her parents, her brother and herself. She was devoted to her mother. When her mother was taken ill and died rather suddenly, Ruth pined silently and died herself about three weeks later. The doctors could find no physical cause for her death, and explained it as shock following the loss of the mother she adored.

It is not possible to generalise. Each child responds in a different way. It is not only the age (and conceptual understanding) of the child; home and family circumstances make a difference; the strength of family ties; the emotional and financial stability of background; the support of relatives; individual personality; spiritual upbringing and the way death comes.

Age and understanding

A baby under six months old, not yet aware of himself as a person, would be unaware of a father's death, and may well be happy with a warm and caring person who would take a mother's place. However, we cannot tell what effect the experience may have in later life.

A Christian lady, who now plays a valued part in church life and is happily married with a growing family, was an infant when her mother died. Her father re-married and she grew up knowing little about her mother, but with a feeling of grief always oppressing her. This persisted even after she became a Christian, until eventually she found a clergyman with a particular spiritual ministry, who identified the trouble and enabled her to find relief. She prefaced the story of how her life had been affected by this early bereavement with some verses from Psalm 139:

> 'You made all the delicate inner parts of my body, and knit them together in my mother's womb. Thank you for making me so wonderfully complex! It is amazing to think about. Your workmanship is marvellous – and well I know it. You were there while I was being formed in utter seclusion! You saw me before I was born and scheduled each day of my life before I began to breathe.' (vs. 13–16 *Living Bible*) I'm sure it's of vital importance to us and to God, what happens to us even in the womb. Therefore what I'm trying to say is that even from conception what happens to us is of significance.
>
> I lost my mother when I was two weeks old and therefore I believe that I must really have sensed the separation and maybe it has affected me. I've had quite a lot of prayer for it – for deep healing – so that memory could be – not forgotten, for we aren't designed to forget – but healed. I used to feel a terrible sense of grief, and I didn't know what it was until I went to a priest, a Catholic monk, who had a healing ministry and he prayed that that memory would be healed.

The toddler has no understanding of death, nor of why her mother does not come to feed her or put her to bed, or to comfort her when she cries. This is a cause of terrible anxiety, and it is most desirable to find someone who can provide a warm, stable relationship to combat the insecurity of such a loss. Up to the age of three or four a child may live for many months hoping for the return of a dead parent, but the effect of such constant disappointment may be tempered by steady loving support from an understanding parent-figure. It may be that the mind of the child will use some mechanism of self-protection to allow her to maintain in her 'inner world' a continuing relationship with the person who has been lost in the real world:

> The children talked easily about their father, particularly the little ones of three or four who made an imaginary companion of him as some children will invent a playmate. They made room for him on the sofa, saved cakes for him, and included him in all their games.

By talking about him in this uninhibited way, the children seemed to spare themselves from the complete emptiness some children suffer through learning to feel – and to say – 'I have no father.' (CRUSE pamphlet)

This is the age when children have a sense of personal power and of being the centre of the universe. If someone he loves dies, a child may see this as a punishment which he has brought about and for which he is to blame. He may feel that in some 'magical' way he is responsible for the death because at some time he has been enraged by the dead person. 'I was naughty, so Mummy has gone away.' A child of four or five may say, 'I'll kill you' or, 'I wish you were dead', but it has no meaning, for the child does not know what 'dead' means. But then if the parent actually does die, the child blames himself and is left with a burden of guilt.

The death of a parent may produce a bewildering tangle of emotions. Not only may he feel guilty and angry with himself, but he may also feel angry with the dead parent for going away and leaving him. Or he may turn his anger on the surviving parent and idealise the dead one, as though trying to make amends. Or it may be God who takes the blame.

Although each age brings its own developmental problems, many of these reactions are common at any age, and we must be prepared for disturbed behaviour. Children are not always able to put into words what they are feeling, and what they cannot express in words may come out in rudeness or aggression or stealing or acts of vandalism. Punishment at such a time is inappropriate, for it has no regard for the hurt that gives rise to such behaviour. Sensitive understanding of the individual child is needed, to think out a way of dealing with the situation that will offer positive help as in this case history:

Manju, a Kenyan Asian; parents and child were in this country for about a year. D.O.B. 1972. Can speak English just well enough to communicate. She is an only child.

Father died suddenly last October just after Manju started school. Mother took child to the funeral and told her Dad would not be coming back.

When Manju returned to school Mother was very upset. I suggested she stay with us and she did this for a little while – for about a week, which helped to resettle the child.

Manju kept saying that (a) the police had taken daddy away, (b) 'daddy is in the ground but soon he will be coming back' and (c) 'my daddy doesn't like me'.

More recently I have found Manju with school property and other children's property in her pocket or in her tray. She has also hidden children's clothes when we get ready for P.E. One example: an item of clothing was missing and it could not be found. I searched in break time and couldn't find it. I asked everyone first before home time if they had seen it and Manju went straightaway to a small chair in the book corner and found it underneath.

I feel this behaviour is her way of compensating for her loss in some way. I tell her why she must not take things which do not belong to her and I try to see she has a painting or a piece of work which she has done to take home. I feel that the child needs time to come to terms with her loss but I will keep a close eye on this tendency to taking things.

Manju's 'naughtiness' is really a cry for help, and fortunately her teacher is obviously alert to this, but if such behavioural problems persist it is best to call in the expert assistance of a child psychiatrist.

Other factors

Death comes in many different ways: it may be after a long and distressing illness, which could involve strangers in the home, or, equally unsettling, periods of staying with relatives. It may come after months in hospital, when the children have had to get used to their father or mother not being around to prepare meals, help with homework, to scold or comfort as occasion demands. It may come with frightful suddenness, as it did to my neighbour's children, when their father was knocked off his bicycle in the traffic and trapped under a lorry. When her father was drowned at sea, Peggy (aged 17) 'had dreadful, disturbing nightmares; seeing her room fill up with water.' Her brother, aged 14, raged against God:

Stephen screamed, 'It's not fair. God could have saved my

Dad. He stilled the rough seas in the Bible. He's not a very nice God.'

The sex of the child and of the dead parent, and the closeness of the relationship are important factors. A girl who loses her mother loses the person to whom she would normally turn for advice over all the different aspects of growing up, how to behave and what to wear, for instance. A seven-year-old girl, watching her father dress in his formal suit with black tie for her mother's funeral, realised the importance and solemnity of the occasion. She knew only that it seemed a time when she should wear her best. Poignantly, she turned to her father for advice. 'Shall I wear my party frock, Daddy?' she asked.

As she grows older she will miss someone to help her with her dress-making at school, and to help her to entertain her friends, to make eclairs and casseroles and go shopping.

Similarly a boy will miss the father with whose interests he would identify; the dad who plays cricket on the beach, makes a rabbit-hutch, shows him how to stand up for himself and kick a ball about.

A significant factor in the development of a healthy personality is the making of a worthy self-image, which helps a child to gain self-esteem and a sense of identity. Parents play a vital role:

> ... healthy personality development in children does depend in large measure on the character of the parents' attitudes and the nature of the parent–child relationship.[6]

It is, therefore, the loss of the same sex parent in particular that makes growing up difficult, and this would be borne out by evidence that a higher rate of delinquency has been found in children who have had to live with the opposite sex parent alone. This seems to hit adolescent boys particularly hard: in a study 'of bereaved in the community the severely depressed bereaved children seem to be mostly adolescent boys who have lost their fathers.'[9]

Adolescence

The physical and emotional changes, peer group pressures, severing of parental ties and the conflicting loyalties, all combine to make adolescence a period of stress, even if there are no other problems. This is the time when the death of a father has the most effect. His was the voice of authority, which, even though annoying, could offer support against persuasive friends bent on trouble. It is not uncommon for a family to break up under the strain of a father's death, as happened to the family whose story is given below. The fact that the bereaved children were adolescents plays no small part in the way their father's tragic death affected them.

> As a family we have not coped well. It was as if Chris was the only thing that held us together and our family life became non-existent. In April 1981 I found out that Peggy (aged 17) was pregnant . . . In June I was in a special sitting of the juvenile court to hear Stephen (14) and seven others receive a caution for shoplifting and receiving stolen goods . . . On my return I heard that both Roy (16) and Stephen, with six others had been arrested after making nuisance calls to my friends. They were found guilty and fined. . . . Roy did not cope with school work . . . Stephen became lazy and very depressed. He would sleep during the day and walk the streets and countryside at night. *Appendix IV*

This family suffered exceptional stress. The father was the respected, much loved head of the family; his death was sudden, (he was drowned when his ship sank in a typhoon off the coast of Japan) and his children were teenagers. There is an immediate warm gathering round little ones who are bereaved, but the response to teenagers is more inhibited, partly, perhaps, because we are not sure how they will react, either to the death or to our sympathy:

> There seems to be plenty of help available for small children but possibly one expects teenagers to cope. This may not be so. Roy (16) told me that during the three days whilst we were waiting for definite news of his dad, he would ride his bike carelessly around the streets thinking that if he were to be killed it would save his dad. Roy's death in exchange for his father's life. (*idem*)

It is not the loss alone of the father or mother that affects the situation. People withdraw from misfortune, they are embarrassed by tragedy. And the change in income may necessitate moving house and changing schools, separating the youngsters from familiar surroundings, teachers and friends:

> Two weeks ago I bought and moved to a new house . . . I knew that I would live in the past forever if I stayed in the house where Chris had been with us. I was totally unprepared for the way we reacted. Peggy was sad. Roy was very sad, Stephen was almost inconsolable and I cried all day. (*idem*)

Children who have an extended family circle are fortunate, for the rallying round of grandparents, aunts and uncles can contribute so much, both in practical ways and in the warmth and moral support that blood ties generate; and often the surviving parent is so distraught that she lacks the resources to give the children the attention they are needing:

> I believe some of the mistakes I made were:
> I tried to be mother and father to them.
> I didn't always tell them how I felt.
> I tried to comfort them when I was in need of comfort, and consequently didn't always cope with the situation.
> Definitely didn't know how to cope with the children's anger that was directed at me. I had to admit defeat and accept that I could not help my children. (*idem*)

The eldest child in a family may often bear the brunt and have to act both as confidant to his parent and counsellor to younger brothers and sisters. A mother will naturally turn to a son for support. He may be told, 'You are the man of the family now', and find this a daunting prospect. He may have to cope with quarrelling younger ones and a crumpled parent while working for a major exam. He may have to take on responsibilities that are the place of a husband, and eventually it may be difficult for him to break away and marry. Similarly a father may become over-possessive of a daughter; or she may have to forego personal hopes in order to 'mother' the younger ones. Bereavement produces circumstances affecting the whole future life.

But although this may force an adolescent into premature adulthood, it is wrong to look at this only from a negative point of view. Luis Palau and David Watson both lost fathers when they were young yet their lives have been richly fulfilled and valuable to others. The child brought up in love and faith may

well reach an unusual depth of understanding and wholeheart-
edly offer comfort to the rest of the family. He or she may find
extra strengths and grow in character. The spiritual background and upbringing are of significance here:

> Life was framed by church attendance on Sunday, Sunday
> School, occasional hymn-singing round the piano on a
> Sunday evening, and 'Lord keep us safe this night' as a
> bedtime prayer. Looking back now I am surprised how
> little I was disturbed by this double bereavement. As it
> happened in the context of war, that undoubtedly helped.
> But God definitely held me steady through the example of
> my mother's reaction and through the Christian teaching
> which had been implanted in my mind by the time I was
> twelve. *Appendix VII*

Early bereavement, although it must affect the circumstances
in which the child is developing and may cause many problems,
need not be permanently damaging. The attitude of the remaining parent and responsible relatives will play an important part
in shaping the child's approach to life. If he can find in them a
firm belief that God is taking care of him, he will be helped to
approach life with courage, faith and optimism. In their turn
these qualities will contribute to his success in achieving a
fulfilled maturity. Moreover, children's wide open, trustful
minds are prepared to a great extent to accept the ideas we give
them – especially our picture of who they are. We must never
give the impression that we are sorry for them. They need our
respect, and we must be ready with praise and encouragement
for every achievement, however small. It would be a mistake to
allow the natural sympathy we must feel to be so evident
during the years when they are growing up that we smother
them with pity instead of making them confident in their own
capabilities. Indeed children with their resilience and inner
resources may cope better than the adult, for they have the
pulse of youth and nature comes to their aid.

Loss of a
child.
6 years later.
The hole is still
there – I've just
learnt to
walk
round
it

7

When death comes to the family

It is not possible to generalise about children's responses to bereavement because every child and every death is different. However, they should always be told the truth when there is a death in the family and included in family plans. It is good to give them encouragement to talk about the experience, about their feelings and about the person who has died. They will do this more easily if adults are prepared to share their own feelings and memories.

'. . . as a little one is comforted by its mother.' Isaiah 66:13 (The Living Bible)

Breaking the news

Death comes in different forms, and each one has its own special pain for those who are left. Violent deaths such as those in the last chapter must be an unprepared and stunning blow:

> My father died about three years ago in a car crash. It happened so suddenly that everyone was in a state of shock. When Mum told me that Daddy was dead, my knees started shaking. I almost fell down.
> My sister Peg screamed when she found out.
> (Peggy and Alletta Laird, aged 11 and 9)[9]

A little later Dad came back to our neighbour's house and took us into his bedroom. He said, 'Boys I have to tell you

something. Your mum died.' There was a loud wail – really loud and really sudden . . . It was such a shock to me.
(Nick Davis, age 15. *idem*.)

Yet one child felt that

In some ways it's easier for me that my father died the way he did – all of a sudden – instead of having to go through a lot of pain and suffering.
(Laurie Marshall, age 12. *idem*)

Another boy had to endure the long-drawn-out trauma of watching his mother die slowly:

When I first learned that my mother had cancer, I felt sorry for myself, but then when I saw how sick she was, I just felt sorry for her. It was painful to see her suffer, but in many ways it prepared me for her death. I mean, it didn't hurt less. It couldn't hurt less. I was just able to withstand the pain more.
(David Harris, age 15. *idem*)

The particular poignancy of childhood bereavement lies in the fact that the very one who would normally be the comforter, is the one who has gone. The one who warmed the chilled hands, quelled the nightmare, raised up the failed examinee, is now needed to help the child to overcome loss and mourn success-fully – needed in vain. The crucial role now falls in double measure on the surviving parent.

Usually it will be that parent who will undertake to tell the children what has happened, unless he or she is too distraught to do so. Then they should be told by someone close whom they can trust. The role may fall to any one of us. Whoever does so, even if distressed, must enter into the entire situation of the child, and care for his physical comfort and bodily needs, for that may help to ease his misery. The heart goes out to the little boy with toothache:

There was a night when I was ill and crying both with toothache and headache and distressed because my mother did not come to me. This was because she was ill, too, . . . And then my father, in tears, came into my room and tried to convey to my terrified mind things it had never conceived before.[10]

The presence of some friend or family member of the same sex as the parent who has died helps to give a framework to span the gap:

> When I told my children their father had died I had both of them sitting on my mother's settee with their Grandad by them (in the middle). I told my father he did not have to say anything, just be there. I told them very calmly that I had some bad news for them, that their father while at work had an accident and had died in hospital. I told them he was up in heaven with God and that he would always be watching us as our life went by. The reaction was instant – tears. Then Graham, to my surprise, wanted to know where, when, at what time. I told him as best I could and then we just kissed and cuddled, my father explained how the whole family would look after us and make sure we were all right, which helped a lot. (*Letter*)

As we have seen, the bonding of babies to their parents owes much to the sense of touch. When the bond is broken there is a great need to seek again that warmth and security of the human touch, in hugging close and cuddling. 'We just kissed and cuddled' is a very natural reaction. It also removes any sense of blameworthiness or guilt.

Another mother wrote,

> When I came home and told the children that their father had died, they sobbed and the three of us hugged closely together. (*Appendix ii*)

This is the time to surround the child with love: to show by word and touch and every evidence of deep affection how much he is loved and cherished. This will enable him to continue to give out love in return, so that his power to make fulfilling relationships will not be impaired as he grows to adulthood. Looking back, a widow remembered how she had a way to help her children:

> Physical contact, a cuddle, a cry, and to admit when I didn't know what happened next, only a firm belief that vaguely there is a reunion at some time. (*Questionnaire*)

And a teacher who had lost her father in childhood recalled

that her support came from 'A very loving mother who knew when to cuddle a child, without saying a word.' (*Questionnaire*)

Telling the truth

Bereaved children need special care: what we do at this time may make a difference to their whole future life. The letters in the last chapter make it plain that some courses of action were helpful, some not. While it is true that what may be appropriate for one child may be quite wrong for another, it is generally agreed that it is best to tell the children the truth, and to tell them at the time:

> My mother died when I was three: and although I am now thirty eight and a mother myself this has coloured my whole life, giving me a fundamentally pessimistic view of the world, which nothing can shift.
> I don't know whether a different handling of my emotions as a child would have made a difference to me, but I suppose it might. My father, from the best of motives, and a desire to spare me, never told me that my mother had died, and never spoke of her. This, I'm sure, is wrong. Before anything else a young child must be allowed to grieve in full. I can't stress too much that however painful it is to the remaining adults, they must encourage the child to experience the full agony of its loss. (*Letter*)

It is not uncommon for children to be sent away when a parent dies, or to be told some story, such as 'Daddy has gone abroad on business' or 'Mummy is staying at the hospital', but children are not deceived by these fabrications. Furthermore, they are left with the feeling of being surrounded by mystery and by adults whom they cannot trust. It is equally unkind to say nothing, and leave them wondering, or to talk over their heads. Truth is also desirable in the case of a parent's prolonged illness. The child is a member of the family and should be included totally in the family situation,

> My father died of cancer when I was eight years old. When he was home I helped take care of him a lot . . . I would fix the bandages around his leg. And I brought him his food. Now that he's dead and I look back on it, it really makes me

feel good that I was able to help him when he was sick – that he could count on me.
                    (Carla Lehmann, age 11)[9]

If a parent is ill for a long time and the situation is not explained, it is bewildering and unnerving for the child, who senses that something is going on, but does not know what it is:

> For us boys the real bereavement had happened before our mother died. We lost her gradually as she was gradually withdrawn from our life into the hands of nurses and delirium and morphia, and as our whole existence changed into something alien and menacing, as the house became full of strange smells and midnight noises and sinister whispered conversations.[10]

When I visited St Christopher's Hospice, I was told how they will gather the entire family into the room where the patient is and allow even toddlers to be present at all family consultations so that they may hear about arrangements which will be made and may have some idea, however vague, of what they may expect. They may understand very little, but at least they know that there are no secrets.

I was told of one small child whose initial reaction to seeing her father so ill in bed, was to hide away behind a chair. After several discussions between the staff and parents with the children present, she gradually emerged and played about the room, growing accustomed to her father's illness and acquiring an acceptance of the situation that would be helpful later.

Simplicity

It is best to make explanations simple and factual. A pre-school child would understand a road accident explained so: 'You know how rainy it has been today. When Daddy was driving home the road was wet. There was another car coming along the road. It was going too fast, not being really careful. Daddy tried to avoid it and skidded into a tree. It was such a big bump that it killed him.'

Or drowning: 'A big wave tipped Daddy's boat over. He couldn't breathe in the water, so he died.'

Or an air crash: 'The aeroplane fell to the ground with such a crash that the people on it were killed.'

Or a childbirth fatality as: 'Something went wrong when the baby was coming and Mummy died. The baby was too little to live without her, so it died too.'

However, sometimes even a simple truthful explanation can produce unexpected complications. One mother told how she explained a stillbirth to her small son, who could not understand how one day Mummy had a big tummy and he could feel the baby kicking, and the next time he saw her there was nothing. She told him that the cord which attached the baby to her had got caught around the baby's throat, so that she choked and died. The little boy did not speak to her for ten days. Then he came into her bed. 'Wasn't the baby naughty, Mummy,' he said. He clearly had the idea that someone was to blame, for later he said that both he and his parents were naughty. Perhaps he was seeking reassurance that no fault attached to himself for jealous feelings when the coming baby had been talked about. This gave the parents a good opportunity to continue talking through what had happened, until there was no sense of mystery or of blame left.

It is important to explain the simple physical reasons for the death for several reasons. In the first place, it can help children to be aware of the physical nature of the universe and the laws which govern it – the law of gravity, the connection between hygiene and health, dirt and disease, the dangers of water, fire and electricity. Even little children can heed such warning. A four-year-old said, 'My uncle died because he just could not stop smoking. I'm not ever going to smoke when I grow up.'

Then, when they realise how death can be caused by carelessness, stupidity and wrongdoing they will be less inclined to blame God, or to hold him responsible for the misfortunes that mankind brings upon itself.

Don't allow your child to grow up holding God to blame for suffering – show them that some tragedies occur through the fault of the people themselves, and others may be the result of natural laws that actually operate to make our world reliable.

For the same reason we should use sensitivity to avoid saying things that might cause bitter feelings in the future. It is also important not to tell children anything that you do not truly believe. One correspondent traced her lifelong agnosticism to such superficial 'comforting'.

Obviously a 'normal' death is easier for both adults and children to accept. Grandmother was old; she had a lovely life; she was very, very tired. (A special sort of tiredness, otherwise the child will panic every time mum says, 'Gosh, I'm exhausted'.) Her body needed a rest for ever; she is, in some way we can't understand, with Jesus. If old people don't die there wouldn't be enough food for the babies – etc., etc. But the 'unnatural' deaths – like my mother's – are difficult even for adults to comprehend, and I do feel that it is a mistake to try to explain them in a religious context to young children (I mean, somehow 'explain them away'.)
(*Extract from letter*)

'That great bully up there'

God does have purposes that we cannot see from here and we must accept, for example, when a wonderful Christian like David Watson dies declaring and transmitting his faith, that it comes within the scope of God's overall sovereignty. But we must try to see this from the child's viewpoint. I used to be unsettled by a poem supposedly written by a child whose mother had died, and who had been told that God had 'taken' her to look after the motherless babies in heaven. The lines,

> Oh, did the Lord forget
> One little child on earth who needs her yet?

used to put me in a cold rage, similar to that expressed in the following extract:

My parents were both agnostics; my mother had been Jewish, my father nominal C. of E. His mother, my grand-mother, was sentimentally, unthinking, nominally Christian, and her attempts to comfort me (from the age of about five) with the idea that my mother was in heaven, and I'd see her later, only served to make me feel extreme bitterness at that great bully up there who had decided that I could do without a mummy. (What did he know about it, anyway? He'd had a marvellous Mum who loved him and understood him – why, she hadn't even gone mad when he stayed away for two days when he was twelve. My dad and granny wouldn't even let me do . . . x,y.z, – whatever!)
Even writing this I'm getting very emotional!
(*Extract from same letter as previous extract*)

If the phrase 'explain them away' means the sort of explanation that would suggest that God 'took' the dead person as an act of callous selfishness I would agree; but this is a complex question. God does work out his purposes through physical causes, and always for our good, and a child brought up in a Christian home with a real faith in God's goodness could accept that on the other side of the great Divide there are still things that he has planned for us to do. Remember the little girl in Chapter 3 who said trustfully, 'Some people die because God needs them to help him.'

Commonsense and perception are called for, and a loving understanding of the individual child. Remember, too, that talking with a child who is suffering the pain of bereavement is totally different from talking about death in the context of everyday living, curiosity and exploration.

Dr Dora Black mentions 'a widowed mother who told her young son that 'Daddy has chosen to go to Baby Jesus in Heaven' and unwittingly left him wondering how one copes with such a powerful competitor.'[11]

It is equally unwise, says Dr Kuhbler-Ross 'to tell a child who had lost her brother that God loved little boys so much that he took little Johnny to heaven. When this little girl grew up she never resolved her anger at God, which resulted in a psychotic depression when she lost her own little son three decades later.'[1]

It is the word 'take' that seems to cause the trouble. In a family where there were three small boys the longed-for baby sister was born prematurely and died. It was a sad blow to the brothers, and one of them suggested that perhaps Mummy might have another baby. 'No', said Andrew, 'if you have another baby, God might take that one too.'

The kind provider up there

There is a world of difference between saying 'God has taken Daddy,' as though that were the cause of death, and saying 'Daddy died of cancer – or in a car crash – but now God is taking care of him in heaven.' The former could destroy a child's faith in God's goodness – only a bad God would 'take' his Daddy, but the latter suggests that God is kind. He provides for us here on earth and up in heaven as well.

The ultimate sovereignty belongs to God but because of the

way he has chosen to relate to his creation the power of the devil is very real. As Christians we have the confidence that God has the final victory.

It should be made plain to older children that the power of evil is no fairy-tale invention, and that many of our sorrows are due to the activities of a personal Devil, who is only too anxious to destroy our faith in God. This is not only true, it is psychologically helpful, for it allows anger to be directed where it belongs, instead of at the kindly Provider, to whom the sufferer should be looking for comfort and help.

> The Vicar said that the sinking of the Derbyshire was no 'Act of God' as Lloyds said but an 'act of the Devil'. Although at the time it didn't offer much comfort, later on it did. (*letter*)

It is not always either kind or helpful to tell a child that her parent died by the will of God.

Reunion

Many childish mistakes will be due to the general tendency in early years to see things concretely, and this will influence the child's idea of heaven as a place:

> Years later she told me she thought that 'Heaven' was a country overseas. (*letter*)

and another child,

> . . . one day when I had bought them a new pair of shoes, she pointed them towards the sky and said, 'Look at my new shoes, Daddy.' (*letter*)

In the family mentioned above where the premature baby sister died, the mother answered the boys' query about heaven with the words of Jesus: 'In my Father's house are many mansions'. She told them, 'It's like when I prepare the guest room for someone to come and stay. He has a place for each of us.'

'When can we go visiting her?' asked the boys, and, 'Then why is baby in the box?' Another child who attended the funeral of his father watched the coffin being lowered into the ground.

'How can he be going to heaven?' he asked, 'He's heading in the wrong direction.' These misconceptions don't mean that we should avoid the subject of heaven with a bereaved child, but that we should be prepared to talk and to keep talking, to help the child accept the finality of physical death, but offer the comfort that although Mummy cannot come back here, one day he will see her again in heaven.

One correspondent who had lost her mother as a child felt that the idea of reunion is irrelevant at such a time:

> To a young child the idea of an eventual reunion is irrelevant – tomorrow is already an eternity away. Even for an adult it is here and now that one wants the loved one. (My daughter, aged eight, has just yesterday come out of hospital – how I envied the other mums who had their mums to lean on, and share the concern with). I'm not sure that the idea of reunion as such is a very scriptural one – and I'm sure that spiritually it is very dangerous, especially for a child. It has to live its life in this world. (*letter*)

There is some truth in this. Like homesickness, it is a pain of the present moment. But nonetheless the promise of a place where we shall meet again does bring comfort to some children, both at the time and as years roll by.

A five-year-old, told that her father was in heaven, was comforted. Her mother wrote, 'One of her first reactions was that she wanted to be in heaven as well.'

Luis Palau testifies to the comfort of knowing that his father was in heaven, when at the age of ten he was left fatherless. The extract which follows pictures a similar foundation of faith:

> A boy in the same class as my elder son, (age seven) has a dying mother. We have spoken many times with our sons about death and heaven as my husband's mother died quite young and his father married again. The comment I wanted to pass on was made when Martin (my son) was in bed and we had said prayers. 'Mummy, if you die, I just can't wait to die.'
> Having told him that heaven is more wonderful than anything we know on earth, and he having accepted Jesus, it was of course a natural conclusion to him. He'd want to go to heaven to be with me if I died! (*letter*)

Secular explanations of death as 'a sleep' or as 'ceasing to be' are not only terrifying, they are false. A child who is told someone 'just went to sleep' may be afraid of going to bed lest a like fate befall him. However confused or limited a child's idea of heaven may be (and adults, remember, do not have all the answers) it can nonetheless offer comfort, and, as it is modified over the years, can make a lifelong framework of hope.

Pray

We cannot rely on our own wisdom in trying to explain to our children those things which we ourselves apprehend only by faith. We have the guidelines of Scripture and we must ask for the words. Children who have been praying for a mummy or a daddy to get well are going to have a big question when that parent dies:

> My daughters always prayed that God would make Daddy better . . . When I came home and told the children that their Daddy had died, they sobbed and the three of us hugged closely together. They asked me why God hadn't made him better and I replied that Daddy had too much illness in his body that the hospital could not make better and so that God thought it best that Daddy went to Heaven where he would have a brand new body and could be happy again.
>
> I was so surprised how the words came out of my mouth, because every time the children asked me a question, God managed to place the answers inside me so that I didn't have to search for the answers. *Appendix ii*

A widow looking back over the years, has found that God not only supplied the answers at the time, but helped her to rear her family to Christian fulfillment:

> They prayed every night for 'Jesus to make Daddy better'. When Daddy went to be with the Lord, Ruth was 5 years old and David just 4 years old.
> I took the children in my arms and told them that Jesus had answered their prayers, and Daddy was now better and had gone to live with Jesus in Heaven . . .

> Ruth, who had only just started school, began to write in her school diary. I found a little note (I still have it) which reads: 'My Daddy is in Heaven, he isn't poorly any more.' As they came through their difficult teens they would

sometimes say 'I wonder what my father would have done or said?' I too wondered this many times, but I have always claimed the promise that He would be a 'Father to the fatherless' and reminded them that they were 'special children' and that the Bible was full of promises for them.

My daughter married a lovely Christian boy and now has children of her own to bring up in the ways of the Lord.

My son has left home and is engaged in full-time Christian work.

I thank God that through the grief and sorrow of losing my young husband the Lord gave me wisdom in helping and rearing my children in a happy home – he does indeed care for us. *Appendix i*

Share your feelings

When there has been a death in the family it is important to establish and maintain an atmosphere of free communication, warmth and unity. It is easy for adults to hide their feelings and withdraw into their own grief. Christians may feel that they should show always a rejoicing face to the world; and indeed we do have reason to rejoice in the hope of reunion in the presence of our Lord. We do not mourn as those who have no such hope; but we do mourn.

In such a state it is difficult to find answers to children's questions. A boy of nine, whose father had blown his brains out, said, 'All my family think he's in heaven, but I don't know.' It's best to admit it when we adults don't know either. But never quench a child's hopeful trust in God.

> For the love of God is broader,
> Than the measure of man's mind,
> And the heart of the Almighty
> Is most wonderfully kind.

However, the object of communication here is not to supply answers. It is to release emotions. We need to provide talking situations and a climate in which the child feels free to express any of his feelings: he needs to talk, not just to be talked to. He needs plenty of opportunities, without feeling pressurised, to talk about his memories of the person who has died, even perhaps some negative feeling about an incident in the past. He will probably feel more able to do this if you are prepared to share your feelings.

A young teenager restrained her own need to talk about her father's death in order to spare her mother's feelings:

> I haven't talked about it with my mother because it would be just another problem for her to think about and she's got so much on her mind already. It's just something else to cope with.

Later she found how valuable real openness could be:

> A few days ago I walked into my mother's room and she was cleaning out everything and she was crying. I tried to hold her. Some other times, before that, when I saw her crying I went in and started crying with her. It's made us closer than we were before.[9]

So it's better not to check the natural response to heartbreak. Some people are upset by children's tears and restrain them, saying, for example, 'Now, now, don't cry, dear', or, 'You'll upset your mother', or 'Be a brave boy.' These are dismissive and superficial phrases. Let them weep without restraint. It is much better for them, and even better to weep with them, too.

> My second point is – don't be afraid to admit your own pain and ignorance (I mean that of the adults involved). Don't try to pretend that 'Everything's all right.' . . . Be honest – and don't be afraid to let the child see you weeping – even Jesus wept at death. (*letter*)

Adults may steer conversation away from the past for fear of making tears flow. But it is bad for a child to keep his feelings bottled up inside. They are nature's healing. He may be encouraged to talk, but this should not be done by cross-questioning. It requires empathy, an understanding of his emotional needs and love:

> The bereaved child needs love, and room to express all its negative feelings, without being rejected or fearing to hurt or embarrass – young children can be very thoughtful and negative. And don't make the awful crass blunder of saying 'Children are so resilient.' Some are – most aren't. Too many adults hide their own fears of experiencing the child's pain under the excuse that children are 'adaptable', 'they

get over things so quickly'. Some might – most don't. (*letter*)

Adolescents sometimes find it more difficult to talk about their feelings than younger children. They are more inhibited, and likely to feel embarrassed by their memories, whether they are happy memories of little affectionate intimate moments of understanding, or whether they are memories of rebellious bitter words and rows. They may feel quite unable to discuss their burden of guilt or anger with anyone. Sometimes they can find relief and satisfaction in writing. They may write down their innermost thoughts and feelings and then tear them up. Or they may enjoy recapturing a memory in words, or writing up a journal of a holiday or special time. Or they may even like to write a letter to the dead parent and burn it.

A teacher was concerned about a young adolescent in her class who had lost his father. He was tormented by memories of furious rows when he had been disobedient and his father had been hard and unyielding. Worst of all, the last time he had seen his father had been the occasion of such a quarrel. His father had kept shouting at him to come and help him on the allotment, but he would not go because he was doing some work. Eventually he decided, when the shouting had died down, to go and pacify his parent. It was too late. His father had had a heart attack and did not recover. At the teacher's suggestion he wrote a full account of the incident as he saw it. He wrote as if he were talking to his father, and explained his point of view. He pointed out why he thought his father had been unreasonable on this and other occasions, but he told him that he loved him and asked his forgiveness. He was able to open his heart and pour out his sorrow, his remorse and his deep unspoken affection for his father. It was a safety valve.

Memories

One of the kindest things that we can do for a bereaved child is simply taking the time to let him talk and talk. Grief finds release in tears, but there are other feelings, sometimes tangled and complicated, that can only find resolution through the filtering of language:

> Having had to console a child bereaved and one facing possible bereavement, the only thing that seemed helpful

> was to allow them to talk out their worst feelings, fears, anger without trying to stop the flow. Repression of these at this time is bad I feel sure. (*questionnaire*)

From another source:

> My brother's elder child, age seven, died, and I think the greatest help to the younger (two years younger) was just talking – finding the right medium in which the child can express her feelings. (*questionnaire*)

And another:

> (Loss of a beloved pet) 'Sitting with the child and allowing him to talk all about it helped: his memories of the pet etc; the fact that the pet was now in a happy place.' (*questionnaire*)

Books and photographs make good talking material and make it easy for the child to talk if he wants to. These allow for a child to talk if he wants to. These allow room for a child to express sorrow, anger or guilt, but do not push him into a corner or make him try to analyse his feelings. Don't put the child under the spotlight – make a way of escape. Looking back through the family album, for example it would be better to ask, not 'What are your happiest memories? Have you any that make you sad?' but 'Where did you go for your holidays? That must have been fun.' One teacher who had had experience of comforting a bereaved child wrote, 'I don't think children should be drawn out to speak about their experience unless they open the subject with you first.'

However, without the use of words, a small child may reveal to a sensitive parent who watches her play, that something is troubling her. It may be that a child between the ages of about three to about five is reacting as described in the last chapter, by blaming herself for a mother's death, and she could be helped by some simple explanation of what actually happened. She could be told that being cross with someone cannot make them ill, or that Mummy's illness was too bad for the doctors to be able to cure it.

 We should encourage children to be realistic, for example about the finality of death, while remembering that this may be beyond the grasp of some little ones. Likewise it is good to keep a rounded and whole image of the person who has died, not an idealised one, though always remembered with affection:

> I believe that drawing attention to the things I admired in him: honesty, sympathy, consideration for other people, a sense of humour, high spirits, a gentle voice, and so on – will help them more than if I never mentioned him. . . . (Of course they know he was no plaster saint. They can still remember his human shortcomings themselves – the fuss he made about going to the dentist, for instance, and the holes he made in the blankets from smoking in bed.)[12]

Keeping a realistic memory alive can make a real support for someone bringing up a family on their own. One widow found that people shunned the subject but 'there was nothing I liked better than hearing about him':

> I made a point of keeping him present.
> Whenever a decision had to be made, whether it was over the family or the job I had to take, I now asked myself, 'What would he have done?' and the answer was immediately obvious. This thought must have crept into my conversation with the children. They also asked me what he would have done.
> When the little ones started school, they went off conscious of their father and as proud of him as if he had driven them himself in the car, as the other fathers drove their daughters.
> . . . Four years have passed and my husband's influence on the family is as strong as ever.[12]

A rounded memory kept alive like this can still give children the example and the model that they need:

> Of course life's a struggle, financially, physically and nervously, but then it always was with all these mouths to feed, shirts to wash and inherited high spirits to control, and when, at the end of the day I sometimes feel like screaming, I remember the touch on my shoulder.
> 'Sit down, love and relax. I'll finish putting them to bed tonight.' I still sit down. I can still relax. And inevitably a few minutes later one of the older children appears with a cup of tea or a smile or both.
> 'Don't worry, Mum. We're getting them into bed.'[12]

8

Bearing one another's burdens

When a parent has died the primary need is to restore the children's sense of security. They should be allowed to attend the funeral if they wish and their daily routine should be maintained. Every effort should be made to ensure that their physical and emotional needs are met. Close links should be established with school, and plenty of activities provided.

There is also a type of bereavement by divorce, and this is an area where the church could make a valuable contribution to the overall care of these needy children.

The Christian who is pure and without fault, from God the Father's point of view, is the one who takes care of orphans and widows, and who remains true to the Lord. James 1:27 (The Living Bible)

In the days immediately following the death there will be all the arrangements for the funeral to occupy the family. Some widows or widowers may feel too distraught to cope with this responsibility and will be grateful to a near relative who will come forward to take it on. But for many this seems to be a last expression of love and they will bring to the task the devotion they feel for the one who has gone: 'I felt that I was still "doing something" for her.'

There is always a lot to be done; and in the hassle it is easy to leave the children outside the circle of discussion, and feeling not only grief for the dead but a sense of exclusion from the living.

> Children are going to be upset as well as the mother and also need comfort . . . not to be told, 'You mustn't say that, it's upsetting your mother,' by some well-meaning aunt. (*letter*)

They should be brought into any discussion, along with the rest of the family and allowed to contribute their ideas if they wish. They can choose favourite hymns and prayers. Which did Mummy like? They loved her too. Would they like to take a bunch of snowdrops? Or pick some flowers from the garden? We know that she is in heaven, but this plot of ground is where her left-off body lies, and so what happens here is precious. Shall we plant a rose?

> When we used to visit my husband's grave, I would tell them it was Daddy's memorial garden. (*letter*)

One 11-year-old was upset when the baby cousin she had loved was cremated instead of buried:

> Christine was also upset that there was to be no grave (though she had no experience of visiting a grave so I don't know why this seemed important to her). I explained that we would always love Jenny and needed no grave to remind us of her, to which she replied that there would be nowhere to take flowers for Jenny. We have a lovely framed photograph of the baby, so we have kept a flower by that, and placed a special arrangement for her there at Christmas, and this has satisfied Christine.
> Recently on BBC's TV 'Songs of Praise' a mother gave a testimony and said she had planted a rose tree in memory of her baby and Christine thought that was a lovely idea, so I expect we will do something about that. *Appendix V*

Children seem to feel a need for things to be done properly, for there to be a fitting end. One of the questions that will undoubtedly arise is whether or not the children should attend the funeral. Parents often feel that the kindest course of action is to spare them this emotional event, and may perhaps send them away for a few days until it is all over. They fear that the service and the rites of last farewell may be overwhelming. However, it is now generally agreed by recognised authorities on children that it is best for them to attend the funeral of someone close, from the age of about seven or even younger if they have been used to church services, if they want to do so.

Myra Chave-Jones, who has had wide experience of counselling adults suffering from neuroses and other problems stemming from childhood bereavement is among those who support this view, but adds the proviso 'if everything is equal', which allows for a variety of factors – the age, personality and the wishes of the child, for instance, and the relationship with the dead person. There is no point if the relationship has not been a close one, for it would not be meaningful; and it would be unwise if the child were excessively sensitive. A child who does attend should be fully prepared by talking about what is going to happen and should be holding the hand of a significant adult, though probably not the chief mourner, and such an adult must be around for a long time to answer questions.

Elisabeth Earnshaw-Smith, who has had the care of families facing bereavement at St Christopher's Hospice, has found that the best approach to terminal illness and death is to maintain complete openness between all members of the family at all ages. Whatever goes on in the family is the business of the child, and she therefore sets no age limit to attendance at the funeral. The child should be included in these critical concerns and secrecy should always be avoided.

A funeral is an occasion when grief can be freely expressed, yet it is contained, shaped and ratified by the ritual and the magnificent words and phrases e.g., 'I am the Resurrection and the Life', which, whether understood or not, have the same quality as music of conveying comfort and assurance through channels of feeling which by-pass the mind.

It is a real experience, far removed from the studied violence and celluloid death of which children see far too much on television.

It is a time when there is a gathering together in sorrow, and the family draws close, so that help can be seen to be available. The child is an integral part of this familial unit and has the right to a place in the common front; left out he may feel excluded from the family gathering, in this crucial moment of his life.

The funeral also helps in other ways – it makes a 'tidy' ending and gives a sense of completeness. It helps a child to grasp the reality, no words needed. It allows the children to feel that what is due has in fact been done. We can recall the distress of the woman whose husband was lost at sea:

> It may seem morbid, but we didn't have a body. There is something 'Monday morningish', a new beginning, about a funeral with a coffin present.' *Appendix iv*

Remember also the need of Christine to 'do something', to plant a rose-tree, to have some memorial, a framed photo or somewhere to visit. A teacher who discussed this aspect with those of her pupils who had known loss wrote:

> Without exception they resented not being allowed to go to the funeral. They loved – therefore no matter how awful the ceremony they should have been there.

> Many were upset because they did not know, or were not told until after everyone else. They were sent to school to be 'out of the way'.

> They liked to visit cemeteries to 'talk' to the dead person (especially if the child is in any sort of trouble).

Although the person may be in Heaven, their grave holds something that once belonged, and like the well-used Bible or the old coat that hangs behind the door, it holds a key to the memory we treasure.

The wisdom of considering the child's own wishes is illustrated here:

> My father was killed at work by falling off a ladder when I was nearly seven years old. My parents were both committed Christians.
> I am glad I was given the opportunity to see Dad's body in the coffin. My nine-year-old brother and I were both given this opportunity. I am glad that I said 'yes' – and my brother is glad that he said 'no'.
> I am thankful that I was brought up in a culture (north east of Scotland) where death was not hidden away but was an event that everyone could share in. Visiting the bereaved, seeing the body (if we wanted to), attending the funeral were all open to children as well as adults. (*letter*)

107

All cultures and all faiths have their own form of ritual for the burial of the dead, from the Viking ship blazing on the ocean to the lofty platforms American Indians build into the sky. Ritual completes the cycle of life: it also makes a significant part of the lives of most people, particularly in the framework it can provide for worship.

It can perform a useful function in the lives of children in the sense of security and perpetuity which it offers. This is true, not only of the funeral, but also of aspects of the life which must now be led in the absence of one of the parents.

Daily routine

Authorities with experience in bereavement counselling agree that it is helpful if a child has been used to some sort of daily routine which can be maintained after the death. Ritual that has been expressed in a pattern of daily prayers is not merely routine, it is a substantial and moral support. Writing in 'The Christian Herald', Luis Palau emphasised the importance of regular family worship, and his advice is impressive when we remember that it comes from the lips of a man who lost his father in boyhood:

> One of the most important ways parents communicate their faith to children is to lead them in family worship. Time for Bible study and prayer should be a natural part of your family life. . . . Prayer is another aspect of family worship that should extend to every part of the day – before school, meals and bedtime. Teach your children to thank God for His protection and goodness. We have a stewardship with every child God gives us. Generally, we have them in our home for only a short time before they leave and establish their own families . . . Make it a priority to say and do those things that will teach your children life's most important lessons.

Home is still the greatest influence on the child growing up: such a family habit as Luis Palau describes is not only a foundation for life; it is also one way in which the routine of the home can be maintained when one parent has died:

> One of the most important things we did, as I look back, was when we started as a family reserving a part of each day

where we could share the Scripture together and pray together. We started doing this as a regular habit in the morning after breakfast before the children went to school and I went to work. So it became part of our daily routine and I'm sure this has paid off very well over the years. It started when the children were very young before my wife died, and I believe that it has benefited the children. It's something which they realise has really helped them each day. So when we had our tragedy we just carried on. It seemed to be the natural thing to do. It is very valuable because any problems you have you can bring out at those times (so can anyone else) and relate it to something God said about it and help those people.

(From a tape-recorded conversation with a father of two children, whose wife died when they were aged eleven and nine.)

It is helpful and reassuring for a child to find that everything has not come to an end. Life still goes on. Breakfast must be at the same time, sports gear must be got ready overnight, someone must cut the sandwiches, iron the shirts and blouses, The very fact that these things continue is itself an affirmation of life.

Keep the home fires burning

The first thing I asked Mom was could we keep Skippy and Shadow, our dog and cat, and could we keep our house, and she said 'Sure'. (Stephen Jayne, age 11)[9]

These words show the importance of knowing that some things will stay the same. Trying to restore the child's shattered security means helping Mom to say 'Sure' to such questions.

First, friends and neighbours can undertake the practical chores that will make it possible for the remaining parent to mourn unhindered. He or she will then be less likely to work out grief through the children or try to make a child the emotional substitute for the lost partner. He can then be helped to help his children, to enter into their sorrow, share his own, pool memories and anxieties and keep the family together.

Friends and church fellowships can free the lone parent of domestic worries, make rotas for meeting the children from school or have them in to tea until their parent arrives home from work. It does not contribute to security to go to school with a key around the neck or to go back to an empty house. Children should never be left in the house without an adult; the fire risk is there, and the fear of intruders.

Neighbours are usually only too ready to rally round taking turns to do the time-consuming jobs with fuses and washers, cooking evening meals, making sandwiches for tomorrow, turning up curtain hems, putting on buttons, mowing the lawn.

Social workers and church communities (house-groups) can be enormously supportive in specific areas of care and in helping to keep the continuity of the home. Keeping the home-base secure is indeed one of the most crucial things. They can explore sources of help if there are financial difficulties or complications about the will or the house.

They can offer moral support in hospital visiting or in troubles that teenagers may get into. Although it might seem that such help would be readily available, the fact is that it can sometimes be dismally lacking:

> I contacted the local Social Services, the Police, the Juvenile Liaison, N.S.P.C.C., the church and anyone that would listen to me, but help was not available. The children were either too old or I didn't live in the right neighbourhood or I hadn't battered them. Help was not available: my family didn't want to know and I became quite bitter. *Appendix iv*

Someone must see to it

Time is one of the major casualties in a bereaved household. A father left on his own may still wish to look after his children himself, but find it impossible with a fulltime job. He may feel that the care of his children is his priority and be prepared to give up his work to do this while the children are small. He could probably receive enough help from Social Security to enable him to do this, but if business or professional commitments are imperative, a grandmother, aunt or close friend may step in. Allowances are available for paid help with the children.

On the other hand, if the mother has been left she may have to forgo a life in the home which she had expected and go out to work. In either case the financial prospects must be investigated through the appropriate channels; but it is the loving care of the children that is the paramount concern. A baby will soon learn to accommodate to the new caretaker provided he or she is prepared to study the infant's needs, maintain the accustomed routine and surround him with love. It is best for the baby to be kept in his own home if possible, and be looked after by one person.

Pre-school children who have been bereaved, especially of mother, may understandably take longer to settle into playgroup or nursery school, and having had one loss, may show a tendency to hang on possessively to the toys they play with, or need more attention from the teacher. Gradually they should be encouraged to socialise in the same way as the others.

Children of school age are growing rapidly and coping with many changes – physical and emotional changes, changes of friends and of school at the age of seven and again at ten or eleven. Their educational requirements must be given careful consideration, as well as their bodily needs and their perhaps rebellious feelings. Are they working too hard? Are they following their natural aptitudes in subject choices? Are they being bullied? Whoever has the overall responsibility must see that the worlds of home and school do not grow so far apart that what is happening in one place is unknown in the other. Someone must turn up at Open Day, and Sports Day, see him win the high jump, or play the 'cello, or watch her play Mustardseed in 'Midsummer Night's Dream'. Someone must take note of academic progress, discuss career prospects or disruptive behaviour. Someone also must see to it that the children are getting a balanced diet and that the child who puts everything into life is combatting nervous exhaustion by getting plenty of sleep; and that there is a quiet place for homework or studying for exams.

The teacher's role

Even though a parent may have died before the child enters school it is still important to inform the teacher of the class concerned for a child may suffer some delayed shock several years after. Especially in a primary school, before the changes in teacher demanded by specialisation, it may well be the class teacher who plays a special part in helping a grieving child. She will have him under her care for most of the waking day, the

111

opportunity to know his ways and build up a relationship of trust. Teachers are uniquely placed to observe how a child is reacting to loss. Understanding the possible responses, they will not punish him for inability to concentrate, readiness to daydream or refusal to participate; and will avoid judgemental comments on reports e.g. 'he only works when he feels like it', or, 'lacks interest in his work'. Alternatively the teacher may realise that the apparently unaffected child may by employing the mechanics of denial to hide the hurt and will help him by a thoughtful choice of stories and plenty of opportunities to chat. The 6–9 year old is more likely to be open about his sorrow than the 9–12 year old. Teachers may help indirectly too by giving the lonely parent their support, introducing him to a circle of friends through the Parent-Teacher Association and finding activities where parent and child can mix socially so neither is left too much alone.

Out and about

Once the first stages of grieving are over, children need to get out and about, to have plenty of opportunities for taking part in sport and activities, finding new interests and hobbies and making friends. Do not forget, too, that a dog can become a real friend for a lonely child, offering silent empathy and the support of unquestioning, unchanging loyalty. Skippy and Shadow, to love and to care for, can fill a large gap. Pets give the child something to be responsible for and offer an outlet for affection:

> I bought my nine-year-old a kitten, which she tended and looked after and loved, and was totally responsible for.

Lots of things to do:

> I filled the house with friends of all ages. She joined an evangelical church, the members of which took a great interest in her. She joined the Girl Guides.

> She wept for the first three months every night and then never mentioned her father again.

> I think being kept busy, active, outward, helped too. (*Questionnaire*)

Friends of their own age can channel children's energies into

112

all-absorbing games; and peer group pressures, which can be damaging in some ways, can also be helpful in the support which friendship offers. This is, however, a time to be watchful that the child who has suffered a loss does not get drawn into undesirable company, and in an endeavour to compensate does not seek it in gang factions or unsocial activities.

The best help that friends can give is to continue to talk about the person who has died. Children can be as embarrassed as adults about offering sympathy, but their silence points up the bereaved child's isolated position and adds to his misery:

> When she went back to school nobody spoke to her about Tom. She wanted sympathy and they acted as if nothing had happened. We all feel this – we want to talk about Tom and so many people can't, so they say nothing. She has a good friend who will speak to her and share with her. She has coped with a change of school work and behaviour has been unaffected by her loss. (Loss of a brother) (*letter*)

Teachers should be on the look-out to integrate the bereaved child in all school activities, to watch for playground loneliness and to correct unkindness:

> The hardest thing to face about my father's death was going back to school afterwards. I walked into assembly and someone made fun along the lines that 'it must be nice not to have a dad'. I know that he did not mean any harm but I got very close to hitting him! (*letter*)

Older friends play a different role; and the inestimable value of the doctor's and church's part in easing pain simply by a Christ-like sharing of suffering is illustrated by these letters:

> We have a very supportive G.P. who was constantly in and out of our house, just as a support, not being able to offer medical help.

> Our ten-year-old son, Thomas, died at home in September after being treated for leukaemia for the past 15 months. My husband and I are Anglicans, and also belong to a small ecumenical prayer group in our village. This group has been a marvellous support and has shared everything with us, and particularly Thomas's last weeks at home. We have a daughter, Anne, aged 13, who after Thomas's death is

'hating God and anything to do with the Church', but is coping with school very well and being loving towards us, Thomas's school friends kept in very close contact with him all the time and particularly shared his funeral, which was a beautiful service of praise and thanksgiving.

A great help to me in the years after Dad's death was the care and interest of other men. There were one or two – particularly in our church's after-church get-together – who played with me and let me sit on their knee. They never took the place of Dad – but they were good friends. (*letters*)

Such friends are a boon and a blessing for a mother trying to bring up teenage children on her own. A man friend or an uncle can speak with authority when the occasion demands, and provide the back-up, in responsibility, leadership and discipline that would have been the husband's role. He can provide the model which a growing boy seeks for his self-image and help him to acquire the practical skills and moral attributes which will complete his manhood. And he can give the fatherless girl some idea of the qualities she would look for in a husband.

It is good to keep photos of the father or mother who has died in the living room or the children's bedroom – in some place where they continue to act as a gentle reminder of the reality of that loved one's existence.

Starting again

Mature friends of the same sex give the adolescent boy or girl who has lost the same sex parent a confidant to whom they can talk about things that may trouble them, and which they feel shy of discussing with a parent of the opposite sex. One teenage girl was relieved when her father found a lady friend with whom she could resolve boy friend problems and experiment with clothes, hairdos and make-up, all of which baffled her father. The need is so pressing that it is not uncommon for children to look around among their acquaintances for a 'suitable' partner for their surviving parent, and to try some match-making, much to the embarrassment of both parties!

Re-marriage does seem at first sight to be the happiest course for the stability of the home:

> Last year my father got remarried to a woman named Ann
> . . . I liked her from the beginning, and now I love her.
> (Gardner Harris, age 16)[9]

But it must not be an impetuous decision: the children may
have their own ideas:

> I don't want them to get married because I know I would
> get mad at John for trying to replace my father . . . another
> reason is because he has children and I know I'd have to
> share my mother with them.
> (Carla Lehman age 11)[9]

> I hope my father doesn't get remarried. My mother was not
> the kind of mother you can replace.
> (David Harris, age 15)[9]

If remarriage is not to be the answer, it could lie in an
organisation, such as they have in the United States, called Big
Brothers which comprises men and women who wish to be
friends with children who have lost a parent through death or
divorce. Links are made between the needy children and the
organisation by guidance counsellors:

> My mother died in September and I got my new big sister in
> October . . . We see each other every week-end and we do
> things like go to movies and go ice-skating. And we go out
> to eat a lot. But the best thing we do is just talk. Meeting
> Mary is about the most wonderful thing that ever happened
> to me.[9]

The children of parents who have been divorced are in much
the same position as bereaved children, and a great deal of
what has been said applies equally to them. Although attitudes
have changed considerably during the last decade, single
parents still do not always receive the immediate sympathy
which naturally is due to someone who has been widowed. The
embarrassment is even more acute. No one knows quite what
to say, and so the lonely parent, who may have been cruelly
hurt, becomes isolated in the home, unable to mix freely in
society.

Myra Chave-Jones has been concerned for many years with
trying to rectify in adults the damage that was done to them as
children by the splitting up of their parents. She believes that a

special share of loving concern should be devoted to these children by the church. It is an area of great need, increasingly widespread, where the responsibility of the Church in some organised or structured form could be enormously beneficial. Alternatively independent parish organisation could be valuable, each house group taking an interest in neighbourhood families known to be in need, whether or not they were already church affiliated. It is best for married couples to take on this ministry of caring; and a lone parent could know that there was always advice or help or a listening ear at the other end of the phone:

> We had been separated, my late husband and I for nearly five months but the shock was still enormous for me and our children. It is one thing when Daddy can be phoned when a problem arises. It is very different when he cannot be phoned. My children and I started going to church after my late husband died. Reverend Brown did the service at my late husband's funeral and instantly I liked him. He has been very kind to me and my children over the past two years, just listening to my problems and trying to help us. (*letter*)

Letters I have received are full of gratitude for the spiritual, moral and practical support of clergy and pastors (e.g. 'With the help of a Methodist minister I was able to sort myself out'), but they do reveal the pressures made on hard-worked ministers by the extent and demanding nature of this ministry. There are helpful organisations such as CRUSE, but they do not cover the whole country. It does seem that this is an area where a church-based organisation of lay people could be valuable. Primarily it is the gift of a listening ear that is needed.

It is by no means easy for us to find the time to listen. Christians have so many commitments. Recently at a women's meeting a single-parent mother confided how much she longed for someone to spend a little time with her and her autistic son. He was a seven-year-old, very far behind in his reading, and what he really needed was someone to hear him stumbling along – someone with patience. It was a warm, welcoming, well-organised meeting of lively women with young families, but it did not seem to have occurred to this needy mother to approach anyone with her problem. I am sure she would have met a willing response, but as there was no system of aid to one-parent families set up, the connection had not been made. She bought two large print colourful books of Bible stories for beginners, in hopes.

Damage
In her extensive counselling experience Myra Chave-Jones has found that 'separation is the single event in the life of a child which can have the most catastrophic effect – the child cannot understand it'. Bereavement does mean loss, but, although it can be damaging, provided things are explained sensibly, a child can see that it is unavoidable and no one has withdrawn from the family unit intentionally. On the other hand, where a mother or father has simply 'gone off', perhaps with someone else, it can be seen as an intentional rejection, a deliberate breaking of the framework of love. However, this may not be the fact where the children are concerned. Children can still be loved when their parents cannot get on together. Arrangements can be such that relationships can be maintained with both parents, at least with some degree of happiness.

In most broken marriages there is likely to be damage to the children, and in some it will be extensive and long-lasting. The sad thing is that children do not put the blame where it belongs. The question in their minds is less likely to be, 'How could my mother/father do this to me?' than, 'What have *I* done? What is there about *me* that has made her/him want to leave me?' However obvious it might be to an adult that the mother has gone off with someone else or that the father's drinking problem was to blame, the child will be likely to find the fault in himself. Cruelly rejected, the boy may become a 'tough guy', hitting out aggressively at a world that has injured him. Or a girl may wonder why her parent loved her so little that he/she went away. 'Perhaps I am not lovable,' she may think, 'Perhaps no one loves me.' And she may therefore find it difficult to form a stable love-relationship in later life.

Binding up the broken-hearted
This is one of the most critical areas in human experience where the Christian message has relevance and positive assurance to offer. First, because we know that even when human love fails, God loves us; and he loves us whether there is

117

anything intrinsically lovable about us or not. Children must be told:

> Jesus loves me, this I know –
> For the Bible tells me so.
> Little ones to Him belong,
> They are weak, but He is strong.

Secondly, we can express that love in our actions, our comforting and the high value we place on each child in our care, or any child who comes within our reach whose self-esteem has been shattered by the loss or the defection of a parent.

A Headmistress has told me of such an instance. A little boy who had a very unsettled background and at the time was living with foster-parents, was sent to her for punishment because of some misdemeanour. She knew that he was very disturbed and often in trouble. 'Why do you do these things?' she asked.

He hung his head. 'I haven't got a real Mummy and Daddy,' he muttered. 'Nobody cares about me.'

'I do,' said the Headmistress. 'I care.'

She could not produce his real Mummy and Daddy, but what he needed she gave him. Somebody cared. He was calmed and comforted.

With all her years of counselling at Care and Counsel as basis, Myra Chave-Jones states that the claims of pressure groups that the one-parent situation does no damage has been belied many times by the problems with which people have come to her in adult life. Often the real strains do not surface until some other emotional catalyst triggers them off. She believes that the Church's responsibility to think and plan for single-parent children should include setting up schemes and seeking ideas that give support, and the delegating of 'back-ups' who would be available to ring at any time. It is so often late at night that children who have played until they are too exhausted or too excited to sleep, bring an anxious and lone parent to the end of the tether.

We cannot take away the loss, but like the Headmistress, we can get across to children the fact that God does care for them and is with them in their sorrows and troubles: that 'when my father and mother desert me, the Lord takes me up.' The nature of God is to comfort as a mother would: our comforting is a picture of God's caring.

Appendices: Case Histories

(1) Telling children aged 5 and 4 of their Daddy's death: a bereavement viewed from the perspective of their maturity.

My late husband was a Pastor and my two children were brought up to talk freely of Jesus and Heaven. They also knew of the Second Coming of the Lord.

They always knew Daddy was poorly, he spent quite some time in hospitals for treatment. He was often a bed patient at home. They prayed every night for Jesus to 'make Daddy better'.

When Daddy went to be with the Lord Ruth was five years and David just four years old.

I took the children in my arms and told them that Jesus had answered their prayers, and Daddy was now better and had gone to live with Jesus in Heaven. They asked if Daddy still needed his walking stick and when I said 'No' they were delighted and ran into the kitchen to tell their Nanny that Daddy was better.

I never ever mentioned the words 'death' or 'dead'. When they saw me packing their father's clothes up to give away, they wanted to know why he didn't need them in Heaven. I told them Jesus had prepared some lovely white clothes for Daddy.

After a week or so they wanted to know when they would see Daddy again. I then told them that when Jesus came back we would see Daddy also.

After another space of days or weeks (I can't remember) they asked when Jesus was coming back and I told them gently that it may be soon or it may be a longer length of time.

I always answered the children whatever they asked and tried hard not to show my grief in front of them.

Ruth, who had only just started school, began to write in her school diary. I found a little note (I still have it) which reads:

'My Daddy is in Heaven, he isn't poorly anymore.'

Years later she told me she thought Heaven was a country

overseas. I had a brother in India at that period of time, who we talked about but never saw, so I wonder if she got the two mixed in her young mind.

When we used to go to my husband's grave, I would tell them it was Daddy's memorial garden.

My little son was always drawing and I found a little sketch he had done of Daddy as he had last seen him in hospital, complete with tubing!

We always talked of Daddy and I've tried to keep his memory alive over the years. I think it was a long time before they realised that Daddy was 'dead', as other children lost grandparents etc. Their class teacher in the Infant class was a Christian and I'm sure helped them over many hurdles. One day, she told me later, she was teaching the children and the question came up about 'Daddy's occupation'. One child said this and another that, in the end Ruth stood up and almost defiantly said, 'My Daddy is in Heaven and has got wings.' (Top that one if you can! Incidentally I'd never told her about 'wings'.)

Now my children are grown up; this was all nineteen years ago. Sadly they have only a very few memories of their Daddy, the rest is what I have told them.

As they came through their difficult teens they would sometimes say, 'I wonder what my father would have done or said.' I too have wondered this many times, but I have always claimed the promise that he would be a 'Father to the father-less' and reminded them that they were 'special' children and that the Bible was full of special promises for them.

My daughter married a lovely Christian boy and now has children of her own to bring up in the ways of the Lord. My son has left home and is engaged in full-time Christian work.

I thank God that through the grief and sorrow of losing my young husband, the Lord gave me wisdom in helping and rearing my children in a happy home. He does indeed care for us.

120

(ii) A mother explains to her daughters, aged 3 and 4 why their Daddy has died, although they prayed for him to get well.

I started going to a Congregational Church in March '82 and my two daughters joined the Sunday School. By September of that year I became a committed Christian and started to talk to my children more about Jesus and the church. My husband wasn't quite on our side and attended church on and off out of curiosity; he wasn't too sure.

A couple of weeks after I became a Christian, my husband found out that he had cancer. Well, he was in and out of hospitals in London for quite a few months with various treatments. My daughters always prayed that God would make Daddy better. (They were nearly three years and four and a half years old at the time.) My husband had more time to talk to God and study his Word, which was a great help when he had to come to terms with the thought of possibly dying. He finally became a Christian and found an inner peace almost overnight. By June '83, things gradually got worse with the cancer and an operation was all the doctors had left to try to get rid of the tumour. This was not very successful and he died ten days later in the intensive care unit. The children never saw him for all the time that he was in the unit and I was hardly ever at home as I spent most of the time I could with my husband.

When I came home and told the children that their Daddy had died, they sobbed and the three of us hugged closely together. They asked me why God hadn't made him better and I replied that Daddy had too much illness in his body which the hospital could not make better and so God thought it best that Daddy went to Heaven where he would have a brand new body and could be happy again.

I was so surprised how the words came out of my mouth, because every time the children asked me a question, God managed to place the answers inside me so that I didn't have to search for the answers. Even though I was deeply hurt I could stay calm with the children. My youngest daughter did not really ask too much, it was Susan, who was then five, who asked lots of questions.

One of her first reactions was that she wanted to be in Heaven as well. She said that she would be a little angel then, as all the children that died were angels, but she didn't know what role the adults played. Then, because he died on the Friday before Father's Day, she said he would not see the card that she had made for him at school. I said that I would place it in his coffin before he was buried. She asked to see his body but I said that it might frighten her. So then she seemed to think that he was a skeleton or monster. Not wishing her to have a bad memory of her father, I explained that he still had his lovely face but because he was ill for quite a while it had become thinner and he had lost all of his hair. (He used to wear a cap or woolly hat most of the time.) I said that she would probably think that it wasn't her Daddy and so I got a couple of photos out and put them in frames so that we could remember Daddy as he was and that would make Daddy really happy. I did not want them to attend the funeral but it has been taped so that they will hear the service when they are a lot older.

Susan kept asking me when I was going to die and they both became very clinging towards me. This lasted for about three months until they felt secure that I wasn't going to leave them. Then Susan wanted to know when she would go to Heaven and would she still be a little girl? I said that she would go whenever God decided she should live in Heaven and that it probably would be when she was grown-up and a mummy herself. She looked very worried and said that how would Daddy recognise her if she was grown-up. I replied that Daddy was in Heaven now with God and she knew that God could look down on us and be all around, that it was the same with Daddy, he could look down and watch what we were doing and how they were growing. It made her very happy and one day when I had brought them a new pair of shoes, she pointed them towards the sky and said, 'Look at my new shoes, Daddy.' Then on Christmas Day we took flowers to his grave as a present and they both stood by the grave and said, 'Look at our new dresses, Daddy.'

My husband used to talk to Susan just before going into hospital and he used to say to look after Mummy. So whenever she did get upset and said that she wanted Daddy (which was not too often), I said that I missed and wanted Daddy too, but as we could not have him we had each other and that Daddy wanted her to look after me and give me some help. They both liked the thought of helping me and looking after me and said that as soon as they get big enough, I will not have to do any housework and I can stay in bed and have a nice rest.

One of my friends told me about one occasion when my youngest, Karen, was having tea with them. It was soon after my husband died. They were saying grace before the meal and their youngest daughter always liked praying for Malcolm, my husband. She was only two and it had not sunk in that he was dead. So as they said grace the two-year-old said, 'And please can you make Malcolm better.' At that, my daughter Karen said that it was all right, they didn't need to pray for Daddy any more as he was better in Heaven.

It has been six months since he died and it does not seem to affect the children at all now. We talk about him a lot and if ever they have friends around from school who do not know about him, my children quite openly point out a photo of him and say, 'That's my Daddy but he has died now and is in Heaven.' They seem happy with the fact that Daddy is with God and that there are others as well for company. It comforts them to know that we will all be there eventually and we can all be together again.

(iii) Children aged 6 and 5 share in caring for their terminally ill grandmother in their own home.

My mother-in-law died in our home in January this year. We had nursed her here for the last few months and she needed a lot of physical care and emotional support.

We have two children aged six and five and they were involved in most of her care and we made them as much part of the situation as we could, given their age and understanding. It was a sad, useful and good experience and memory for all of us and the children seem to us to have gained, not lost, from it.

Derek and I are both nurses so she came to live with us as she did not wish to go into hospital but needed a lot of physical care. We explained to the children that she would not get better but we would look after her and keep her comfortable. They knew she would die – 'like their tortoise had'.

We made the dining-room into a bedroom for Imogen. The

children helped choose with her what we put in it and as Christmas was coming they helped decorate it for her. However, we ensured they had space to play elsewhere (they used to use this room), and the chance to make a noise upstairs.

We both work (me three nights a week) so had to work a system of rotas so that someone was around with Imogen all the time, but tried also to make sure that at some point in the day one of us took an hour off with the children to go out and let off steam – vital for all of us.

Friends were very vital to give the children an alternative place to play, especially during the last two weeks when Imogen could not cope with their noise when they were restless. We found that an hour elsewhere morning and evening were the best, rather than longer periods. (Maybe they wanted not to go away for too long.)

Ruth was five and a fairly lively but motherly girl who enjoyed helping make Imogen's bed, rubbing heels and giving drinks – even holding vomit bowls on occasions. Terry was a more concerned six-year-old not keen on helping physically, but he would hold a drink and straw and happily read bits of newspaper items or talk and look at photographs. He enjoyed writing cards and drawing pictures to stick near Imogen and fetch and carry for her. They were around her most of the time, by their own choice, but left the room if they wanted to watch TV, listen to tapes etc. They didn't ask a lot of questions about death or illness. In fact they were bored by the subject.

The last three days or so they got quite fed up with the amount of time it was taking to care for Imogen and they did not like what she looked like. So they opted to go out more often and spent less time with her. They expressed anger and resentment, and we let them. It seemed healthy. We explained that Imogen would die soon and she was very uncomfortable, so we did have less time for them, but it would not go on for long.

They understood I think that cancer is an illness which harms the organs ('bits') of our body and so they gradually stop working. They were told that it would not spread to them, and that the medicines would help her not to have any pain, stop being sick etc. They were not with her when she was incontinent or when we gave her injections.

When she died they were out playing with a friend. We

brought the children back to the house so that they were with us and saw the funeral company arrive with the coffin and remove Imogen's body. They went to the Funeral Chapel to see Imogen's body a few days later. We were going and asked if they wanted to come. They did, but found it boring after a few minutes. Ruth did not approve of the lacy clothes, which she said Nana would never wear – so she re-arranged it to look less lacy. Terry liked the Funeral Chapel lighting arrangement. They understood that some people who were very sad liked to come and sit here for a while and think of all the happy times they had had with their relatives. We did not stay long!

The funeral they attended with us. The service was simple and they understood the child-orientated sermon. Ruth enjoyed the limousine. Terry the food afterwards. Both thought the attractive crematorium was OK and were pleased that the service was short. Afterwards they talked little to us about any of it – more keen to do things that they had not been able to do recently. Their younger cousin who visited occasionally did play 'dead' occasionally, and get someone to send for a coffin. We gather they talked to friends at school and 'explained' death to them. They did not appear to do much grieving afterwards, and do not talk much about it to us.

Recently there was an Open Day at the crematorium and they went with Derek to look around. They were interested in the facts of what happened and seemed to appreciate seeing what went on behind the curtain. We had explained cremation as (a) Nana's choice and (b) she no longer needed her old body. She had a new one which was not ill.

I think they are more aware of life having an end and what old age means. They have had the experience of having to put their needs aside and consider someone else more. They do not seem in many ways to have been affected at all. They are still as noisy, lively and take as many risks, still 'kill' each other in fights etc. Terry is thoughtful and talks of heaven occasionally, but he was more thoughtful anyway. Ruth is more aware and thoughtful than she was – but maybe she is just older.

We appreciate that it would not have been possible to care for Imogen without their cooperation, and value the experience as a family memory that was not bad. They do know they will see her again and have occasionally said, 'We'll have to ask Nana. She will know now.'

I think their acceptance was a help to us. Their normality and ability to switch off Imogen was good for us – made us realise the world was still going on. However, trying to keep them quiet and amused on occasions added more stress and meant that we could not rest when Imogen was resting. It was vital that Derek and I were working together in it and talking about what to do next.

(iv) The father of teenagers is drowned at sea: the break-up of a family.

My husband, Chris, was a Chief Officer on board the m.v. Derbyshire. We had a varied life. Chris was away for about four months on board ship and then would be at home for about two months. We had recently started attending a church and, at different times, had given our lives to the Lord. We had daily Bible readings together as a family and many discussions. Chris decided that he wanted to 'do something for the Lord' and so resigned from his job. We were accepted as foster parents and hoped to run a children's home together. His notice expired the end of August 1980 but his leave was over in June. Chris was an honourable man and so joined the ship 20 June 1980. He never returned. On or about 9 September 1980 he was drowned or killed when the ship sank: all forty three people on board were lost. It was thought to be as a result of a typhoon (Typhoon Lotus) and happened about three hundred miles off the coast of Japan. Chris was 42 years, the same age as myself. Peggy was 17 years (born 18.2.63), Roy was 16 years (born 3.5.64) and Stephen was 14 years (born 27.6.66). I also had two foster children at the time.

Most people said at the time what a blessing that the children were older. I disagree. Smaller children would have accepted more easily that Daddy had died and gone to heaven.

Peggy had dreadful, disturbing nightmares; seeing her room filling up with water. Stephen screamed 'It's not fair. God could have saved my Dad. He stilled the rough seas in the Bible. He's not a very nice God.' Roy said nothing and wondered what all the fuss was about.

Their various peer groups were mostly admirable and very supportive. Occasionally, Roy's friends were unkind but this was dealt with quite adequately by the school.

The first year was sad but not as bad as the next two. As a family we have not coped well. It was as if Chris was the only thing that held us together and our family life became non-existent.

In April I found out that Peggy was pregnant, in May '81 my father-in-law died and in June '81 Peggy married Paul. In June '81 (actually 20 June 1981, exactly one year after I had seen Chris) I was in a special sitting of the juvenile court to hear Stephen and seven others receive a caution for shoplifting and receiving stolen goods. (Stephen met the shoplifters and was given a tube of lipsalve). In November '81 Michael was born to Peggy and Paul and he brought us great joy. In July 1983 I bravely (and tearfully) set out on my first holiday alone. I felt physically and spiritually improved. On my return home I heard that both Roy and Stephen, with six others, had been arrested after making nuisance calls to my friends, neighbours and strangers. In December 1982 they were found guilty and fined.

By this time I had very few friends left. My father, mother-in-law and my brother were very silent about the affair.

Peggy has continued to attend and take an active part in church, Roy went occasionally and Stephen not at all.

I believe some of the mistakes I made were:

I tried to be mother and father to them.

I didn't always tell them how I felt.

I tried to comfort them when I was in need of comfort, and consequently didn't always cope with the situation.

Definitely didn't know how to cope with the children's anger that was directed at me.

Roy did not cope with school work. He left after completing only one year in the sixth form. He enrolled for a two-year business studies course at the local college and managed to pass. His attendance was poor but he managed to pass the final exam. with a poor result (disappointing, as his tutors described him as brilliant). Fortunately he has been able to enrol at a Polytechnic for a degree course. His behaviour deteriorated so much during 1983 that I gave him an ultimatum. Change your behaviour or get out! And I meant it. He changed! Quite dramatically too! Since starting at the Polytechnic in October 1983 he has become quite friendly and co-operative. He also had time to sit and think, and to think about his Dad. At last he has been able to grieve: painful but beneficial.

Stephen became lazy and very depressed. He would sleep during the day and walk the streets and countryside at night. He was dismissed from one 'Y.O.P.' job by being late for work. His insomnia became a serious problem. A visit to the doctor was unhelpful, but a large jar of Horlicks and new flannelette sheets had some good effect. Stephen has fortunately commenced, in September 1983, a year's computer course run by the M.S.C.

Two weeks ago I bought and moved to a new house, just two miles from our old one, where we had lived for 10½ years. I knew that I would live in the past forever if I stayed in the house where Chris had been with us. I was totally unprepared for the way we reacted. Peggy was sad, but she has her own home now, so it was less traumatic for her. Roy was very sad, Stephen almost inconsolable and I cried all day.

But we have moved, we will look forward and I thank God for a sense of humour, my gift from him.

It's easy to look back and think and see what I should have done. I feel that special counselling would have been of benefit to us. It may seem morbid, but we didn't have a body. There is something 'Monday morningish', a new beginning, about a funeral with a coffin present. The two memorial services we attended did not compensate for this. (The one in our local church, the other in Liverpool Cathedral arranged by the company.)

I was unable to maintain a high level of discipline when it was needed. I contacted the local Social Services, the Police, the Juvenile Liaison Bureau, N.S.P.C.C., the church and anyone that would listen to me, but help was not available. The children were either too old or I didn't live in the right neighbourhood or I hadn't battered them. Help was not available: my family didn't want to know and I became quite bitter.

I had to admit defeat and accept that I could not help my children. This was a turning point in my life. I decided if I couldn't help them, then I would help myself.

With the help of a Methodist minister from another town – I

travelled 25 miles to see him – I was able to 'sort myself out'. I had been a daughter, a wife and a mother for a long time and now I was ME. But who was ME? With the help of some very positive thinking and a lot of prayer I began to assert myself. This had some beneficial effect on the children.

We are at the beginning of a new life now. It isn't all roses of course. In fact, at this moment, I'm struggling to find even one small bud. But we are trying to look forward.

The one thing we have always agreed about is that Chris is in heaven and that has been a great comfort to us. Stephen continues to be very angry with God – it still wasn't fair. Several people told Roy that now he was the man of the house; he couldn't cope with this and so he opted out and did nothing. People even told me that I would remarry (some even said that I should). This did not help the children either and they strongly told me that I wasn't to remarry. I believe they were made to feel very anxious – quite unnecessary as I have no desire for remarriage.

There seems to be plenty of help available for small children but possibly one expects teenagers to cope. This may not be so. Roy told me that during the three days whilst we were waiting for definite news of his dad, he would ride his bike carelessly around the streets, thinking that if he were to be killed it would save his dad – Roy's death in exchange for his father's life.

The teenage years are a traumatic period anyway, without coping with the death of a parent. I was interested, though, in the fact that Roy made friends with boys who also did not have a father.

(v) The birth and death of a handicapped baby girl: the response of the other children

My sister and I live close to each other, and between us have four children: Christine aged eleven, Robert aged eight (my children), Gavin aged seven and Hilary aged four.

We have a very close relationship, the children feeling equally at home in either house, often spending the night together, holidaying together etc. Mary, our husbands and I became Christians in our early teens and are still members of the Baptist Church we joined then. The children have been brought up in Church from their earliest days, and are all at various stages in the Sunday School. Christine gave her heart to the Lord Jesus at a Covenanter Houseparty in August.

We all looked forward with great excitement to the arrival of Mary's third baby, the children having made gifts and helped with the preparations. However, baby Jenny was born prematurely in April, terribly handicapped. Her brain had failed to develop, leaving her with physical deformities (a tiny head with severely receding forehead, scarcely any nose, bulbous eyes, and a cleft palate). She was blind and deaf, with no voluntary movement, had to be tube fed, was unable to control her body temperature, and had fits. Although her life hung precariously on a thread for the first week or so, her physical condition stabilised, and only a month later she was allowed home, though the consultants warned that her life expectancy was low (four–twelve months at most).

We loved her dearly, sharing her between the two families to ease the burden of care. She brought out an immense gentleness and patience not seen before in the children, who never once even appeared to notice her appearance as anything out of the ordinary. To each child we explained what we could of her condition, warning them that we should not have her very long. We read together *Angel Unawares* by Dale Rogers, wife of the American Roy Rogers, the 'Singing Cowboy'. The book was written as though by the baby concerned. It told of how God had decided the Rogers family needed to learn certain truths so that they could be more use to him, so he sent an angel on a short mission to earth, who took the form of a mentally handicapped baby born to that family. When her job was done she returned to God, leaving the family sad at the parting but glad that their baby should have been so used by God. We have often talked about it since, and it was a real comfort to us to know that God had planned Jenny's life and loved her, just as he planned and loves the other children, that every step of the way she was in his care and keeping, and that it was through our reactions to this experience that her life would have value and meaning.

Jenny died at the end of August, just a day short of four

months old. The girls wept, the boys remained dry-eyed but quieter then usual. We wanted them to treat death as naturally as birth, so allowed them to see Jenny's body in her cot and her coffin, though Christine chose not to, saying she would rather remember her as warm, soft, sweet-smelling and alive. Robert remarked later that it was funny to see someone not breathing. He had thought she was just asleep until he had noticed that her chest was not rising and falling. We talked about how she did not need her body any more, so had left it behind, and told them that the real Jenny who had been inside all the time but could never have grown and blossomed in that body, was now perfect and complete in heaven with Jesus, and that while they grew up here, so she would be growing up in heaven, and that one day we would all be together again in heaven. We read the last pages of *Watership Down* in which the rabbit leaves his body behind. (My children subsequently saw the film at Christmas and Robert came home and said that he was glad that had happened to Jenny, because it didn't hurt at all.)

A day or two after her death, Hilary and Gavin were arguing about who was going to have Jenny's toys – in particular both wanted the musical mobile which had been sent from Singapore. In several ways they seemed almost callous and uncaring, but if they believed what we had said, then logically why should they be sad? Christine showed a great deal of distress at the fact that a post-mortem was held, and also that Jenny was to be cremated. She kept asking, 'How can they do that to her?' I don't think she has ever really come to terms with that, though we explained that the post-mortem might provide the doctors with clues to help other babies to live. Quite recently she said again that she still couldn't understand how Aunty Mary could have let them do that to her own baby. Christine was also upset that there was to be no grave (though she has no experience of visiting a grave so I don't know why this seemed important to her). I explained that we would always love Jenny and needed no grave to remind us of her, to which she replied that there would be nowhere to take flowers for Jenny. We have a lovely framed photograph of the baby, so we have kept a flower by that, and placed a special arrange-ment for her there at Christmas, and this has satisfied Christine. Recently on BBC TV's 'Songs of Praise' a mother gave a testimony and said that she had planted a rose tree in memory of her baby and Christine thought that was a lovely idea, so I expect we will do something like that.

It seemed natural and right that all the children should attend the funeral, and we emphasised the aspect of saying, 'Thank you' to God for the time we had spent with Jenny, and for all the good, loving things that had come out of the whole experience of facing up to her handicap and death.

In the week after the funeral, Hilary was overheard telling an elderly neighbour that her sister was in heaven, and assured her that we had been to heaven to visit her, proceeding to describe the undertaker's Chapel of Rest where we had seen Jenny in her coffin! The same neighbour told Hilary that the baby was now a little angel, flying round in heaven, to which she replied with disgust, 'Don't be silly, – she's only a baby – she can't even walk yet!' Just before Christmas she asked Grandma, 'Do you know whose birthday it is on Christmas day?' When she replied, 'You tell me,' she said, 'Jesus's – and this year Jenny will be going to his party.' On several separate occasions she has made remarks like, 'I wonder what Jenny's doing in heaven today.' Whereas the older children have, in some measure, a concept of a spiritual life after death, Hilary's ideas are entirely concrete. I remember that Robert at a similar age said that he thought heaven had fitted carpets so that when you fell you never grazed your knee.

(The lady who wrote this letter later said of the baby's mother):

She wanted to stress how well her children have accepted all that has happened, which we put down to the mountain of prayer which was raised by the Church on our behalf. We had heard of other children becoming severely disturbed after bereavement and needing professional help and guidance; and also of children being afraid to go to sleep (Jenny died peacefully in her sleep) for fear of not waking up again, but none of these things happened. Perhaps the fact that they had been well prepared for Jenny's death, and that we tried to be open and keep talking and encouraging them to talk, helped.

Mary also wanted to stress the way her children talk and seem to think of Jenny as continuing to live, but as it were in a different room. They talk of her often, and still clearly regard her as part of the family. If asked how many sisters he has, Gavin continues to say, 'two'. This is not through nonacceptance of the fact of her death, for he is equally clear in explaining that 'she died, so she now lives in heaven.'

The story of Jenny's four months and the wonders of God's love in that time would make a book in themselves . . . The first Sunday after Jenny was born our pastor preached on the healing of the man born blind (John 9). When Jesus was asked whose sin had caused the handicap he answered: 'Neither this man, nor his parents sinned, but this happened so that the work of God might be displayed in his life.' (John 9:3 NIV). All that has been done and said has been with that aim. Then, of comfort, has been Psalm 30:5 (NIV): 'Weeping may remain for a night, but rejoicing comes in the morning.'

(vi) Answering a three-year-old's questions about her father's death

My husband died in November last when my daughter was aged three years three months. My husband had been ill for a year (he had leukaemia) during which time he was in and out of hospital. We moved to the area from Edinburgh in October 1982 shortly before my husband was found to be ill. My husband's family actually live in the area. Until March last year we hadn't got our own home, and so lived with relatives. All this, I felt, added to the trauma of the situation, and therefore when my husband died I was worried about my daughter Katie's reaction.

I needn't have been. I received and still receive a great deal of support from my church. The pastor advised me to tell Katie of her father's death as soon as possible. The opportunity came that day when she asked me if I was going to visit daddy. It was easier than I expected – we had always been open with her although we had felt that my husband Tim would get well again, and so I thought it would be a great shock to her.

From the beginning she accepted it well. In fact a few days later when I was having a weep she said, 'Never mind Mummy, you'll see Daddy in heaven.' Shortly after this on my refusal of sweets she retorted, 'I am going to take a Milky Way to heaven and share it with Daddy.'

From the time of my husband's death until fairly recently Katie and I talked about him daily, always instigated by her. I feel it has helped us both by being open and talking when it seems right. There are many occasions when Katie seems to be old beyond her years in accepting it all. However there have been times when I haven't been able to answer her questions, but the Lord prompts me and an answer comes.

Recently, on sorting out my husband's clothes, Katie asked what would happen when her daddy rose up again with Jesus – he would only have his pyjamas. I told her not to worry, I am sure God would give him a new suit with his new body. She does think of all the practicalities.

Obviously she does miss her father but she has accepted it all well. Whenever any stranger talks to her about him she gives them the facts e.g. someone remarked on how tall she was. 'Is Daddy tall?' she was asked. 'My daddy is dead,' she replied candidly. I do not discourage this openness although I know it is embarrassing for the person concerned.

Katie is very interested in the Second Coming, and looks forward to seeing Jesus and her daddy again.

I found that I haven't helped her, but the reverse, she has helped me with her simple faith. We have been helped enormously by our church, and Katie, in particular, by her Sunday School, which she loves.

(vii) **A wartime bereavement of a twelve-year old: the influence of a quiet Christian home.**

There were five of us in the house at the start of the air-raid. My mother and I, aged twelve, were the only two who survived it. So without the preparatory sorrow of seeing loved ones unwell. I had to face the death of my healthy father, only sister and grandmother.

The fact of heaven was definitely of the greatest value to me in my actual longing for my father and sister. I somehow came to the straightforward realisation early on that it was selfish of me to want Daddy back, as where he was in heaven was so much better than this world. And that thought just seemed to settle the matter. Heaven for me was, thankfully, a reality – and that made all the difference. This was consolidated by the way that the Guide magazine noted my sister's death – it was briefly recorded under the heading 'Called to Higher Service', with the Gone Home sign, and that just strengthened my matter-of-fact knowledge of where they were.

I don't think that the Christian hope of re-union entered much into my thoughts, it was as if I knew that they were in the 'best place', but life for me was full and happy so I was quite content to carry on down here, and not think about the future.

Looking back now I am surprised at how little I was disturbed by this double bereavement. As it occurred in the context of war, that undoubtedly helped, as death was no stranger. But God definitely held me steady through the example of my mother's reaction, and through the Christian teaching which had been implanted in my mind by the time I was twelve.

(viii) School phobia and bereavement: an unusual response

I was eleven when my mother died. I can remember her very well. She was a quiet person unless she was with people she knew, and she was kind and loving. She was a Christian. We went to church about twice a week and at breakfast time we all had a Bible-reading and prayer time and every night we had a prayer time before we went to sleep, before bed. I went to Sunday School, and from a baby I went to church with my mum and dad.

I hated school and had a lot of trouble at school. I didn't like to be away from my mum and I found I was ever so shy. I felt safe with my mum – it was fear.

My mother was ill for a long time. First she had shingles and she was in bed for a long time with that, then she got a bit better. Then she was ill again and I didn't realise that she was seriously ill. She went into hospital, and I thought that she'd be coming out soon. I only thought she had back trouble. I didn't realise that she had cancer.

I had no idea that my mum was very ill and two nights before she died I had a dream. I dreamt that something was going to happen to my mum. I didn't know what, but something serious was going to happen. It could have been God's way of warning me. I can't remember being very shocked by it.

At first it was not as bad as what we might expect. We had a lot of Christian friends and relations around. I really sensed that God was with us and he really helped us through it. It didn't seem to affect me in a big way really.

I went to the funeral and remember sitting next to my grandma. We had the minister come from my old church and he took part in the service, with the minister from our present church. I remember afterwards seeing my relations whom I hadn't seen for a long time, and friends that I didn't see very often had something to eat in the hall at the back after the service; and I remember relations came back to our house. The thing I remember was that I saw the relations who weren't Christians crying, and I didn't see the Christians crying.

I had used to keep running to my mother, clinging to her. I wouldn't let her go. After she died I could face school. The teachers and friends at school just couldn't believe it, because before I used to really hate school and used to be really upset when I had to leave my mum. I used to have a lot of trouble at school: but I was all right. My friends were good to me at school and my last year was my best year at school. I had used to cry at school because I hated it so. I was a very nervous child. I think they thought I'd go to pieces, my mum dying, but I didn't. I didn't even cry any more at school.

I still had my fear of school, but I was able to cope without having my mother. I started to realise that God was really real, and I knew that it wouldn't be the last time I would see my mum. I would see her when I went to heaven. I knew she was a lot better off. She's really happy now. She hasn't got any pain, and I didn't see much point in being sad.

I understood what heaven was: I imagine it up in the sky, but I know that it's a good place where there's no more pain or fear and everyone is happy. Jesus – God – is there, and the ones you've lost will be there.

I think if I hadn't been taught about heaven before I'd have been very confused and it would have taken me a long time to accept it. I don't think I'd really have understood. I remember the night mum went into a coma, and all that night I prayed to God that if it was his will he'd let her live, but if he wanted her, to take her. I didn't feel resentful. I felt my prayers had been answered. I think it was God's will for her to be with him in heaven – what he wanted. There must be a reason why God takes people when he does. When people tell me about someone they've lost, I understand exactly how they feel, because I've been through it. But if I hadn't had the experience I wouldn't really understand. I've shared this experience with others.

I was a Christian before my mum died, but it was after my mum died that I realised how real God was. We couldn't have got through it without him. We'd have gone to pieces.

(ix) Guilt and anger: danger signals overlooked

My husband died seven years ago as the result of a car accident. It was rather sudden inasmuch as he went off to work one morning and didn't come home again. My children were seven and ten years, both girls.

They attended Church/Sunday School regularly. The eldest child had given herself to the Lord and in fact through her prompting my husband and I had only been committed Christians ourselves for one year before he died.

Therefore my reaction at the time was to be thankful that he knew the Lord as his Saviour and was sure of a place in heaven.

In fact I remember saying 'even if Daddy could come back he wouldn't want to because being with Jesus is better'. This caused false guilt within my children because they were angry God had allowed their Daddy to die. Yet the impression I and so many other Christians gave them was that they should be glad. A mistake so easily made yet with regrettable consequences. I now know I should have talked with them getting them to express what they felt.

Both children reacted differently. One flew into fits of anger especially when I had to go out and leave her, I had a battle to bring her to allow me to go out in the car. In hindsight I see she had a fear that I too may crash and not return home.

137

My younger child withdrew and in many ways suffered more because she was so quiet no one took any notice. Her progress at school came to a halt yet again. It wasn't seen at the time; only years later was it realised by her immaturity.

What I am trying to say in all this is that I had no idea of the danger signs. The signals my children were sending out were ignored not wilfully but simply not recognised. I didn't know how to work through grief with my children by spending time with them, talking, maybe just sitting quietly with them. I was so determined to get through a day at a time and relieved when I did so.

(x) A father tells his children of their mother's death – a 'precious experience'

We are a Christian family. Janet and I married in 1952 and right through our married life we sought to bring up our children in the way of the Lord, believing as Scripture said that if we train up a child in the way he should go, when he is old he will not depart from it. And so we sought in our way to follow what the Lord wanted. So when it came to 1967 when Janet was very ill that obviously created some difficulties in the home and the family.

Joanna was eleven and Jeremy was nine at the time. I wasn't a hundred percent sure that the children had been informed as well as they should have been, but there are times in life when we have to commit our children to the Lord in faith. There comes an end to the way we can protect our children. We were aware of the prayers of Christians.

The problem was that the children were at school and I had to go and tell them that their mother had died. I went and met them from school and we walked home across an open green area at the back here – the sort of place you go for a game of ball, somewhere the children always liked to go. I sat us all down on the ground. I didn't quite know what I was saying but I realised that God was here where we were and that all I had to do was just communicate with him. I didn't know how to tell the children. I just asked the Lord to do it, to help me – and I was absolutely amazed! That seemed to be one of the most precious experiences of my life. The children showed no obvious emotion – concern, yes – but they seemed to be so much at peace, and so was I. Peace seemed to be overwhelming us at the time, and it was such a precious experience just to share that.

I've gone back to that place a few times and every time I do I find myself almost weeping and just praising the Lord. Often at night I just stand there and I lift my hands and my heart up to heaven and I just praise the Lord. Because I realise he did something very special for us that day.

(xi) Dying children

Speaking on television recently Dr Elisabeth Kuhbler-Ross said that dying children are more spiritual than other children, and have a better acceptance of death. Life after death is confirmed by young children, who will tell you, that 'Mummy and Peter are waiting for me.'

In her book *Suffering in Childhood* (The 1979 Barnardo Lecture) Dr Janet Goodall has included the words of a father who was 'able to share the way in which he and his wife had parted from their child':

> Her eyes had closed and it seemed that this was the end. Then to our surprise . . . she began to experience a gradual transformation . . . Her eyes began to dance and shine with delight and astonishment at something she could see and we couldn't and she asked why it was that we couldn't 'see them singing' . . . We were privileged to see her gradually becoming aware and awake to another world . . . Eventually, whilst placed on my lap . . . she snuggled up . . . She was very content and her heart stopped beating and we knew that she had gone into the presence of the Lord . . . I don't feel that any parent whose child has died in these early years needs to feel anxious about their welfare *at all*.

That father's assurance is confirmed by another parent whose child also caught a glimpse of heaven, and I have before me the actual word-for-word testimony of his 12-year-old daughter who was dying of brain cancer. I have not been able to trace her parents for their permission, but I believe they would wish to share this, as they wrote that it gives forth the testimony of a child as to the reality of heaven:

> Mommy, I want to tell you something. Sit down by my bed. Last night Jesus came to my room. He really did. You won't be able to believe it, but it's true. There was a wonderful bright light just as if the sun started to shine in the night. I saw Jesus with his arms stretched out like this. He was saying 'Come.'

Notes

1   Dr E. Kuhbler Ross, *On Death and Dying*. Tavistock Publications (1970).

2   Diane Baumgarten, *Melissa*. Triangle (1980).

3   Kenneth Howkins, *Religious Thinking and Religious Education*: A Critique of the Research and Conclusions of Dr R. Goldman. Theological Students' Fellowship (1966).

4   Kenneth Howkins, *Teaching about the Exodus*. Religious Studies Today, Vol. 7, no. 3 (Summer 1982).

5   Earl A Grollman, *Explaining Death to Children*. Boston (1967).

6   Ed. Witmer and Kotinsky, *Personality in the Making*. Harper and Row (1952).

7   John Inchley, *All about Children*. Coverdale House (1976).

8   Ron Buckland, *Children and the King*. Scripture Union (1979).

9   Jill Krementz, *How It Feels When a Parent Dies*. Gollancz (1983).

10   C. S. Lewis, *Surprised by Joy*. Bles/Collins.

11   Dr Dora Black, with the help of CRUSE staff. *The Motherless Child*. CRUSE Pamphlet.

12   A widow, *Father's Place*. CRUSE Pamphlet

Bibliography

Gladys Hunt, *Don't be Afraid to Die*. Zondervan (1971).

Jill Barbara Menes Miller, *Children's Reactions to the Death of a Parent*. Journal of American Psychoanalytical Association (1971).

Michelle M. Van Eerdewegh, Michael D. Bieri, Ramon H. Parilla and Paula J. Clayton, *The Bereaved Child* British Journal of Psychiatry (January 1982).

Averil Stedeford, *Bereavement*. Medical Education (1983).

Stuart Lieberman M.D., L.M.C.C., M. R. C. Psych., *Living with Loss*. Postgraduate Medical Journal (October 1982) 58, pp. 618–622.

The Child and Bereavement, from the Paediatric Collection of St Christopher's Hospice.

Dr Alfred Torrie, *On loving your child*, CRUSE Pamphlet.

Some helpful books for those who have been bereaved

Joseph Bayly, *The Last Thing we Talk about*. Scripture Union (1970).

Harold Bauman, *Living Through Grief*. Lion Publishing (1983)

Peter Cotterell, *Death: your questions answered*. Kingsway (1979).

Charles Ohlrich, *The Suffering God*. Triangle (1983).

Cicely Saunders, *Beyond All Pain*. SPCK (1983).

Jean Richardson, *A Death in the Family*. A Lion Guide (1979).

Eugenia Price, *Getting through the night*. Triangle (1982).

Sources of help

CRUSE, the National Organisation for the Widowed and their
Children, CRUSE House, 126 Sheen Road, Richmond, Surrey
TW9 1UR (01–940–4818/9047) has branches throughout
Britain and offers counselling and practical advice to all
widowed people.

The National Council for One-Parent Families, 255 Kentish Town
Road, London, NW5

The Compassionate Friends, 2 Nordon Road, Blandford, Dorset,
DT11 71T

The Stillbirth and Perinatal Death Association, 15a Christchurch
Hill, London, NW3

National Council for the Single Woman and her Dependants, 29
Chilworth Mews, London, W2

The Dayspring Group, 180 Bexley Lane, Sidcup, Kent
(01–300–5920)

Samaritans, Citizens' Advice Bureaux, Social Services, General
Practitioners and Health Visitors, teachers and schools, Child
Guidance Clinics and Child and Adolescent Psychiatric Clinics